LANTERNS *in the* DARK

A Holistic Guide to Navigating Special Education Without Losing Your Sanity

Rebe Goebel

Lanterns in the Dark: A Holistic Guide to Navigating Special Education Without Losing Your Sanity
Copyright © 2026 by Rebecca Goebel

Published by: Freya's Haven LLC

St. Louis, Missouri

www.rebegoebel.com

First Edition: April 2026

Paperback ISBN: 979-8-9950011-8-8

eBook ISBN: 979-8-9950011-0-2

Audiobook ISBN: 979-8-9950011-1-9

Library of Congress Control Number: 2026908504

Cover and interior book design: Jon Hahn Design
Cover photo: Vlad Bagacian / Pexels
Edited by Dawn Raffel and Jamie Strauss
Printed in the United States of America

CONTENTS

Part III: ABCs and IEPs—Everything You Need to Navigate the School System

Part IV: Essential Skills—You've Got This, Mama!

Part VI: References & Resources

INTRODUCTION

You look up one day and stare at your spouse. With a lump in your throat, you say, "I think we need to get our son tested for a learning disability or, I don't know, a behavior disorder or something. I think he needs help." But because no one talks about it, you have **no idea** who has travelled this path before you and **zero** clue where to start. Do you start with your pediatrician? Or with the school? You have no map to guide you in this foreign land. You just know it's complicated, could potentially be messy, and you really, really want to hide under the covers and pretend it away.

It likely started with an email or a note home from preschool, daycare, or the elementary school. Or maybe it was a quick, distracted conversation at drop-off or pick-up. Maybe you've noticed that your child's grades are slipping in one specific area. Or when you stop to think, you realize it goes **way** back to things you noticed early on - that whisper in the back of your mind telling you your kid maybe isn't quite the same as others.

Regardless of how it starts, I've been there. Twice, as a matter of fact. My husband, Alex, and I have two children: Max and Henry, who are both in high school as I write this. They each have enough special needs to require specialized support from our family, the medical community, and their schools. However, unlike other children, their needs are not obvious to a casual observer, which created additional challenges in getting both the family and the school to agree they need help. I started out thinking this would be a smooth process. I just assumed the school would automatically work closely with us to provide the services we were requesting for Max. Little did I know how wrong I was. Alex and I were about to embark on the fight of our lives to get what we **knew** Max, and subsequently Henry, needed to succeed.

After an extremely rocky start to the process with our oldest, I realized I needed to get smart *fast.* I did just what I'm guessing you've done – I looked around desperately for a map to guide me. I could find plenty of books with advice on different ways to parent my kids. There are tons of books on what it's like to have a child with a specific medical condition. There are even a few technical, legalese-heavy how-to books on getting Individualized Education Programs (IEPs) set up. However, I couldn't find a comprehensive guide for *me.* As the parent, the one who has to do all the things, be the adult, and deal with all the other adults, where should I start? What should I expect? What role should I play in the process? How do I pull everyone (family, medical professionals, the school, special education, etc.) together to form a team? How do I get that team to work **with** me and **for** my child? How do I even find out about resources? And at an even more basic level, how the hell do I care for myself while doing all of the above? What does self-care look like when I've just been pitched headfirst into survival mode?

That book, the one leaving me lanterns ahead on this strange new path, didn't exist.

If you're lucky, you know someone who was in a similar situation or who maybe works in education and can give you a fuzzy idea of how this process works. I was able to turn to a friend who had briefly worked in Special Education in another state. She knew enough to get me started and then called bullshit when things went sideways for my family. She didn't have all the answers, but she lit that first lantern for me and she connected me to others who could give me more guidance. But in case you don't have a friend like I did, I've written this book to show you what's ahead on the path.

Exceptional children are given to exceptional parents.

I know you just read that line about exceptional parents and rolled your eyes so hard you nearly sprained them. I don't blame you. If you're anything like me, I know you don't feel exceptional. You feel wholly inadequate, stressed, short on time, and desperately lacking patience. You may have a full-time job, other kids to take care of, a household to run, your sanity to protect, a dog that needs to be walked, and a spouse you want to connect with every once in a while. Your plate is full. I totally get it.

But I know no one else understands my children like I do. I know no one else loves my children like I do. And I know you feel the same way about your kids or you wouldn't have ever picked up this book. I am the mother my children need me to be, because the stakes are too high and failure isn't an option. So I simply am. You are, too, or will be soon.

I am a trauma-informed Parent Advocacy Coach. My career and this calling were born out of a desire to teach all the things I've learned over more than two decades of professional and personal experiences to other parents just like me – the ones just trying to get their babies the support they need. Over the last decade I've successfully advocated for my children and built not one but roughly ten different teams for my boys across two states and the different schools within our district. Together with my husband, we have worked through significant con-flict with difficult school administrators and their lawyers, navigated transferring an IEP from one state to another, moving from an Early Education IEP all the way through to high school, and we are currently looking at what life looks like for my oldest after graduation. After a lot of work, I believe we have a great relationship with our current schools, the school district, and the Special Education community, and I'm finally confident my children are receiving the services they need in a positive environment.

In order to achieve this, the first thing I had to do was change my mindset. I thought I was being active and engaged, but in the one way that really counts, I was a passive participant. Things didn't turn out well for us in that very first meeting because I walked in expecting to find out what the school had decided to do for my child. I didn't go into that first meeting ready to play a role in making that decision. I had given all that power away and as a result the school denied our first request to evaluate Max.

It didn't matter that I had a wealth of professional skills to draw on. I started out as an officer in the Air Force, which gave me countless lessons in leadership, including how to create high-performing teams in crappy situations, and how to be poised under pressure. I also have fifteen years of experience negotiating multi-million dollar contracts with some of the largest companies in the world. I've managed teams — I know how to keep a project on schedule and monitor milestones, be organized, communicate clearly, and develop and track metrics.

I knew all those things, and I was good at my job. And yet, we still stumbled in the beginning with Max because we were passive players during those first few months. Eventually, I put all of these skills into play in order to achieve the <u>only</u> outcome that was acceptable to us — getting our children the support they need to thrive in school and achieve their version of success.

That may sound daunting to you. You may be thinking, "I don't have all those skills! Am I screwed??"

But here's the great news — 1) It's your active participation that's critical, and 2) They're just SKILLS.

That means anyone can develop them. You, Mama, can learn how to do these things with a little bit of guidance. This book will teach you how to travel this path with confidence, get the supports your kiddo needs to be successful, and not burn yourself out in the process.

While this book is meant to be more "how-to" or guide than memoir, I believe there is value in hearing other families' stories and learning from them. *Lanterns in the Dark* is divided into six parts, which you can read in any order you like (but please, whatever you do, do not skip Part II "Sanity-savers You're Going to Need"). First, "Our Story" introduces my family and the struggles we've had to overcome. It will show you how I've put some of the critical skills I'll be teaching you to use during the process of building teams and getting the right support structures in place for each of my children.

Part II "Sanity-savers" focuses on you, your mindset, your self-care, and the foundation inside your home with your partner. The fact of the matter is that this path you're now on is one of those 100-mile ultramarathons. If you don't start with supporting yourself, who will support your child(ren) when you go down? Trust me, **self-care is critical to your survival**. I also completely understand how quickly we get to the point of rationalizing that "peeing in uninterrupted solitude" is our self-care for the day. This section is filled with wildly practical and effective practices that can be done in literal seconds. There's a reason why it comes before the rest of the book.

Part III "ABCs and IEPs" provides an overview of the timeline from "I think something is wrong and Billy needs support in school" to "Whew! That's a big, fat checkmark next to Finalize IEP!" This section touches briefly on getting medical support, but its main focus is working with your school. You'll find worksheets to get you ready for each meeting available in the extra book resources on my website. When a piece of my story helps illustrate a point, I add it in along the way. I want you to truly understand when I say I **know** what you're going through; I really, really do.

Part IV "Essential Skills" is really where we hit the meat of this book – the skills you need to develop in order to successfully build a team, communicate effectively with them, get and stay organized, and negotiate and advocate like the warrior-mama (or papa) you are. You will inevitably get tired and encounter people who don't understand what you're going through, so I've also included tips on dealing with unhelpful people in your family and wider social circle.

Next you'll find Part V "Practical and Sustainable Self-Care." Here, we will go over systemic, long-term changes you may want to make to reclaim some of your energy and sanity. You'll learn how I consider what to do, delegate, or delete from my task list. I will share ways to stay positively connected to your partner, other children, extended family, and your community. I will also share how to handle holidays or other family gatherings, as well as what to do when people aren't as supportive as you'd hoped for.

Finally, I've included Part VI, a "Reference and Resources" section. Here I've included a list of all the resources available on my website, *http://www.rebegoebel.com/bookresources*, along with some quick reference lists of the strategies outlined in "Essential Skills."

I want you to know, right down to your toes, **you can do this**. There were times I felt totally lost and completely overwhelmed. I've raged to the skies. I've been sure I wasn't strong enough to handle both what my children and the school were tossing at me. I've cried while washing the dishes and had to step back from more than one rant-filled email before I hit send. I want you to know all those feelings and reactions are normal, but they will pass. You will figure it out. You will get your kid on the right combination of therapy/support/meds/etc. for them. You are going to get the help you need for yourself and your child, and you are so, so much stronger than you think you are.

Okay, Mama. Take a deep breath and let's get to work. Just follow the lanterns I light along the way.

PART I

OUR STORY

Looking back, with that clear 20/20 vision hindsight affords you, I can see Max was born exactly who he is. We probably should have known when the teacher in his daycare's infant room, with 30 years of experience under her belt, told us it had been a long time since a baby had given her a "run for her money" as Max had. Max was constantly moving even before he started crawling, but since he was our first, we chalked his antics up to being a high-energy boy like his daddy, and life moved on.

When Max moved into his daycare's classroom for two-year-olds, they started to work on skills like keeping your hands to yourself and how to stand in line. About halfway through the year, his teachers started mentioning concerns about his behavior. Eventually, there were enough instances of Max being impulsive, hugs turning into wrestling matches with peers, his inability to stand in line, and his struggling to express himself that his teachers asked Alex and me to come in for a parent-teacher conference.

The blur of time has erased many of the details of that conference, but I remember how odd it was to be in the daycare midday. During naptime was the best time to speak with both his teachers at once, and the juxtaposition of sitting on tiny chairs in the corner of a darkened classroom while children slept with the gravity of our conversation struck me. I was also late in my second high-risk pregnancy, which added complexity to my thoughts and feelings that day.

It's hard as a parent, especially a relatively new parent, to sit down and listen to someone tell you there is something wrong. As the one who handled all the drop-offs and pick-ups at the daycare, I had more opportunities to observe the behaviors his teachers were telling us about. While I immediately went into "okay, how do we fix this?" mode, Alex started asking a lot of questions about how Max's behavior differed from that of the other children in the class. Initially, I felt defensive and embarrassed by his approach with the teachers, but they were actually really good questions. I still use them to this day, and I recommend you keep them in your back pocket, too (more on that in "Essential Skills").

In the end, we agreed to do some private evaluations for sensory processing issues and speech delays through a group that already came into the center to work with other kids. We figured the evaluations wouldn't hurt and could only serve to provide us with more unbiased information than we had. The recommendation came back to us that Max would benefit from speech therapy and occupational therapy for his sensory-seeking behaviors (he needed more input from his environment to feel "satisfied" — the hug turned into rolling on the ground, chewing on everything, etc.). This is the opposite of sensory avoidance, where people are easily overwhelmed or overstimulated by their environment.)

We agreed to both therapies through this private company and began keeping a close eye on his development. At the time, I didn't know we could have gone through the school district or one of the other early childhood support resources available for free through the school district. However, given that those services are provided in your home school district mid-day, and Max was in daycare onsite at my office, which was 30-45 minutes away depending on Chicago traffic, I would still have chosen to pay for his therapy out of pocket. I'm thankful for and recognize what a privilege it was to be able to make that choice.

Max was only in therapy for a year or so, but he continued to need some accommodations for "wiggle-breaks" and we worked hard with each new set of daycare teachers to educate them on his needs. I started checking in with the teachers at the end of each day to make sure I had a real-time view of how he was doing in the class – again, always asking the question, "How does Max's behavior differ from what you would expect to see from a child this age?" to make sure we, as parents, had the right perspective.

As daycare became more like preschool, with less play and more work, we had to work harder with Max and the school. We also had to get more creative with the supports we requested for his classroom. He attended the same daycare for kindergarten, where he did well in a smaller classroom with kids and teachers who had known him for years. However, we knew going into first grade at the local elementary school that he would need accommodations and perhaps individualized support to be successful.

1

MEET THE GOEBELS

BEFORE I GET TOO FAR AHEAD OF MYSELF, let me properly introduce myself and my family. Then we'll get back to the kiddos, okay?

My name is Rebecca, but please call me Rebe, which sounds like Debbie with an R. There is a lifetime of stories I could tell you about growing up in the Midwest, attending the University of Missouri, and meeting the love of my life, not to mention the too-crazy-not-to-be-true stories every parent has once their children get a mind and will of their own. But for our purposes right now, you might like to know that, in addition to having two children, an uncle, and a cousin with special needs, I have a unique understanding of the situation we find ourselves in…I had special needs, too, as a child. At the age of ten, every joint in my body was stiff and swollen, and my eyesight began to rapidly deteriorate. After a long series of doctors' appointments and testing, my parents discovered that the nine strep throat infections I'd had two years prior had entered my bloodstream, causing a condition now known as infectious arthritis. In the mid-80s, though, that diagnosis didn't exist, so the pediatric rheumatologist was stumped by my symptoms. At eleven and twelve, I was old enough to remember everything…all the doctors, the regimen of medication, the impact it had on my activities and friend-ships, and the fights my parents had over how best to help me. And I vividly remember my mom going mama-bear, fighting a school and the 1980s-era school system that wasn't yet even trying to be inclusive and supportive of children who needed more than "average."

I know firsthand how incredibly important it is for you, as a parent, to work well with the school. Trust me when I say that, even though it shouldn't, a poor relationship with your child's teacher will undercut the quality of support and consideration they get in the classroom. This knowledge, felt as a child and confirmed as an adult, has given me a deep passion for helping other parents be the best possible advocates for their children.

Luckily for me, my little body fought back and, after five rough years, I had very few lingering physical effects from my illness. I'd say it was very lucky, because through a few other twists of fate, I found myself applying to the Air Force Reserve Officer Training Corps (ROTC) Program on campus as a college senior, just a year away from graduating *summa cum laude* with a degree in business.

A few days before my senior year started, I walked up to the "Welcome New Air Force Cadets" sign hanging next to a smoking grill and table laden with burgers, hot dogs, chips, and soda, with sweat running down my spine. Both the thick, mid-August air and my nerves were wreaking havoc on me, and I nearly didn't go up to get any food. But then I caught a flash of a million-watt smile on a tan face. I turned to get a better look (I was 21 and single after all) and the handsome young owner of the smile that still makes my knees weak waved me over.

Neither Alex nor I had any clue just how pivotal that moment would turn out to be as he introduced himself. It would take a while for us to start dating, but we quickly knew how well suited we were for each other, and we married just months after my graduation and commissioning as an officer.

Alex graduated and received his commission six months later, and we set off to begin our active duty careers as a Contracting Officer (me) and a Communications Officer (Alex). The military taught us both a lot about resilience and making the best of it when you find yourself in a crappy situation. We learned how to communicate effectively and advocate for those who worked for us. We learned how to take ownership of the teams we led and how to take care of the people on those teams and show them they're appreciated.

As many two-officer couples discover, the military is hard on families. Once our initial commitments were over, we decided to enter the corporate world, and both found jobs in Chicago. Alex worked as a consultant and then became the Director of an IT Internal Audit team.

While neither of those jobs is glamorous, both solidified his skills in improving established systems, leading and managing teams where he wasn't the boss, and made him scary-good at evaluating the success (or failure) of a program.

For my part, I transferred the contracts and negotiation skills I'd developed in the military right over to negotiating multi-million dollar contracts for both Motorola and BP America. As a young woman, I routinely sat across the negotiation table from 60-year-old male CEOs or business owners. These experiences provided me with invaluable lessons in how to interact with others, sharpened my negotiation and analytical abilities, and forced me to develop serious long-term project and program management skills.

We also started our family while in Chicago, welcoming Max in 2008 and Henry in 2011. I loved being a mom, but happily returned to work after taking a generous maternity leave, placing the boys in a great daycare co-located in my office.

While I will finish detailing our two experiences navigating the confusing and often frustrating world of getting educational supports and services for our children here in just a moment, it makes the most sense to jump a bit ahead in my personal timeline so you understand why I'm writing this book and what I hope to achieve.

After nine years in Chicago, we moved our family to St. Louis, and I decided to try my hand at entrepreneurship. Running my own business quickly took a back seat to the growing needs of my children, and allowed me to become a leader within the special needs community in St. Louis, serving five years on the Executive Council of the Special School District Parent Advisory Council (PAC), including three as President.

Many of you reading this will find that your child's school district is responsible for providing both general education and special education services to all children who reside within its boundaries. However, St. Louis, along with roughly two other places in the country, is unique in that special education services have been carved out from the 22 school districts in St. Louis County and are provided by an "umbrella" organization called the Special School District. As part of the PAC for this overarching organization, I represented over 24,000 children who were receiving services and partnered with members of all 22 school boards and their superintendents to increase the supports and resources available to our children and their families.

It was during this time that the idea for this book was born and the first drafts were written.

Then the COVID-19 pandemic hit. I was the President of the PAC at the time, trying to navigate my own children being home with no support services, and also representing all the other families who were in the same situation. Add to this my own anxiety, plus helping my mom as my dad's Alzheimer's symptoms become unmanageable at home, plus not knowing what the education system would even look like when all was said and done… Something had to give, and so I quietly closed this file on my computer and stepped away.

During this time of anxiety, grief over the eventual loss of my father and then my 94-year-old grandmother, and the stress of moving my mother across the state so I could care for her as well, I cannot overstate my gratitude for finding and working with an amazing life coach and somatic healer. I'd tried therapy, and while it helped me a bit, the soul-deep healing I've been able to do since the fall of 2020 is exponential in comparison. With my work in the field of special education on pause, I dove deep into learning about the nervous system and became a trauma-informed breathwork facilitator. I went deep down the rabbit hole of all things metaphysical, opening an online crystal boutique, becoming a Reiki Master, and getting certified in somatics, hypnosis, and life coaching.

Now, before I lose you here, let me say — This book is NOT about spirituality. But I'd be lying if I didn't say that the tools I've learned are absolutely foundational and have made me a happier, better person. That, in turn, allows me to show up for my children, my mom, my partner, and myself in a way that's aligned with who I want to be. I am more effective every time I interact with the school because I'm not walking in dysregulated with my emotions all over the place. I am grounded, calm, and confident when speaking with administrators and, what I need you to hear is that **you can be, too.**

Over the last five years of focusing on neuro-science and somatics and working with clients, this closed file – this book that was probably already 85% written – was still on my mind. I know, with soul-deep certainty, that this book will improve your ability to navigate the world of special education. But as a business owner, my focus was elsewhere, and circling back to this project felt like a side quest, a distraction. What I realized a few months ago is that, as I've woven these nervous system and mindfulness practices into my life, I'm more resilient and have handled the bumps and persistently stressful situations with more ease than I ever have.

I started to wonder, what if the foundation of it all – building a team that works with me and in the best interest of my child, getting the support we need, and being a solid family unit – starts with me and my nervous system?

What if the key isn't knowing the IEP process or the fancy negotiation skills or any of the knowledge in my head, but how well I take care of myself first, so that I can do all the things from a full cup?

What if self-care isn't selfish at all, but a matter of survival for all who depend on me?

What if I could rewrite this book, sitting on the proverbial shelf gathering dust, and share how, with the short and wickedly efficient self-care practices I use, you can walk into your own child's school cool as a cucumber and increase your ability to advocate even if you learn nothing else from this book?

Let's get back to Max and Henry's story, and then we'll find out together, shall we?

2

WHEN IT ALL
WENT SIDEWAYS

So, we left off with me realizing, towards the end of Max's kinder-garten year, that I probably needed to call the new school to have things in place for him. I called the principal (who we'll call Mrs. Taylor), and shared with her about his sensory seeking behaviors, history of speech and occupational therapy, and his need for classroom accommodations like the option to use a standing desk, tying an elastic band around the legs of his chair at his regular desk so he could bounce his feet against it, and frequent movement breaks.

I specifically asked if we needed to do any formal evaluations so he would have everything he needed on Day One of first grade. She made all the right noises of assurance and promised me they could accommodate him in the classroom with no formal IEP needed. The school regularly made adjustments for kids, she said, promising me, "Nothing you've told me about Max worries me. We've got him in good hands, Mama."

That conversation took a huge weight off my shoulders! I breathed a sigh of relief and dared to look forward to the next school year. Right away, though, he started to struggle. Practicing ten spelling words for his weekly test took 45 minutes, and he had at least two meltdowns each time. His handwriting and reading skills were below average for his age. He was literally chewing through everything he could get his hands on, like pencils, water bottle tops, the plastic containers I sent in his lunch,

16

and even a metal zipper on his hoodie. Reports started coming home from both his before and after school programs that he was "aggressive" and not being safe with his body. And then in November, we started getting a lot of emails from his teacher. Max was being too rough on the playground. Max was not focusing. Max was disrupting others in the class. Max couldn't sit still. Max got sent to the office.

Toward the end of January, when Max's second-quarter report card and formal reading test results came home, we knew something was wrong and that the "standard" in-class accommodations and supports the principal was sure would work were not sufficient. Max was struggling too much with behaviors at school and at home, plus we could now see that he was falling further and further behind academically. We spoke to a friend, Amy, who had worked in special education in Indiana, and she encouraged us to formally request evaluations from the school district.

I found a template request letter online, typed it out, and dropped it in the mail, naively confident that the process would flow smoothly and Max would get what he needed.

Oh, sweet summer child. I had no idea what I was in for.

We got a response back, setting up a meeting at the school. Alex and I cleared our work calendars and went in looking forward to learning about what the school was going to provide above and beyond the "standard" things they were already doing. The reality of that meeting was very, very different.

It all started out fine. We went over the months' worth of emails we had exchanged with his teacher. The behavior issues. His grades. How he was falling further and further behind his peers. All eight attendees at that meeting spent an hour agreeing with us – we were all seeing the same things at school and at home. There were nods all around.

And yet, I have a crystal clear vision of the conference room at the very moment the principal said, "So, at this time, I'd like to inform you that your request to have Max evaluated by the school district for special needs has been denied. We will keep an eye on him and discuss this again if he starts to fail." With that sucker punch delivered, she snapped her folder shut, stood up, and walked out.

Stunned by the unexpected outcome of the meeting, Alex and I found ourselves quickly ushered out of the school. It wasn't until we hit the parking lot that my brain kicked back into gear.

"Wait….WHAT?!?!" I stopped square in the middle of the sidewalk and turned to Alex. "What the hell just happened in there?!?" Clearly as shocked as I was, he stood there shaking his head.

"I…I don't know. I thought we were all on the same page and were just going in to talk about **which** tests to do - not **if** testing was going to be done! But I definitely don't agree with their decision. What do we do now?"

He looked at me like I had the answers. Ha, ha, ha, yeah…not so much. I was just as clueless as he was.

I'm so incredibly thankful Amy texted me that afternoon, asking how the meeting had gone. As I filled her in, the fury rose in both of us. The school's decision was utter nonsense, and we both knew it – but I didn't yet know just how bad it was.

I hadn't yet taken the time to really get smart on our rights, Max's rights, in this whole process. What was guaranteed to him by law? What was available if I just knew enough to ask for it? I only knew that, to fight the school, I was going to have to become smarter than they were about the process, their responsibilities, and my child's right to a Free and Appropriate Public Education (FAPE).

Amy put me in contact with another one of her friends who has children with special needs and is an Educational Advocate who helps other parents fight for their kiddos. She told me, "The school just called your bluff. You found that standard request letter on Google, didn't you? Yep, and you cited a bunch of regulations and federal law in the letter without reading them first, and the school knew it. So they've denied your request, hoping you'll leave it at that because they know you aren't really educated on the system. Otherwise, you'd have called BS during the meeting. Now we've got to start over. Here's your homework assignment, Rebe…"

Determined and fully in warrior-mama mode, I bought the book she recommended (listed in References and Resources) and spent every lunch hour for a week reading it cover to cover. I started printing all the emails and notes I'd kept from every phone call and gathered all the report cards and testing results we had, and I got myself organized (see Chapter 16 "Organization"). Last but not least, I typed out a new letter, requesting (again) that Max be formally evaluated for special needs and dropped it off personally with the secretary.

The next day, my phone rang. "Mrs. Goebel, I received your letter yesterday, and I must say I'm a little confused."

"Oh? What are you confused about, Mrs. Taylor?"

"Well, it appears to be nearly the same letter you sent me a month ago, requesting that Max be evaluated. I don't understand. What's going on?"

"You're right. It is nearly the same letter. Alex and I don't agree with your decision, and it appears we've been steered in the wrong direction a bit here. So, we'd like to sit back down with you and your team to discuss Max's need for evaluation. Again." I said calmly, but firmly.

Mrs. Taylor reluctantly granted our request for a second meeting, and this time, I walked in ready to be an active participant in the decision being made and to use every single skill I possessed to get the school to work with me. Yes, I was royally pissed at the principal, but I also knew I needed the people who would be interacting with my son daily to have respect for me and how I handled myself in spite of the obvious conflict.

This time, I knew I needed to set a different tone from the beginning if I wanted to achieve a different outcome. I stopped at Panera to purchase a dozen bagels and a carafe of coffee. *(Subtext: See! I'm on the same team as you! Let's work together.)* I wore a suit. *(Subtext: I'm on an equal level of power and professionalism as you.)* And I walked in with a massive 3-ring binder already half full with documentation. *(Subtext: I am prepared to discuss this request in detail, and I have the receipts to back it up.)* I wanted to make it clear to everyone in that room that I had done my homework since the last meeting, and I was serious about getting Max the support he needed.

The school finally agreed to test Max, but they made things difficult for us every step of the way. I brought an advocate to one meeting that Alex couldn't attend, and the principal refused to hold the meeting because we didn't notify them in advance. We asked to see documents before meetings so we could be prepared, and they gave them to us as we walked in the door. After it was determined that Max was **indeed eligible** for an IEP under multiple eligibility criteria (for his diagnoses of ADHD, Sensory Processing Disorder, and a Learning Disability in the area of Writing), they then challenged our right to provide input on the IEP goals they had proposed for Max. We insisted on reviewing the goals and asked for a follow-up meeting with the individual authors (for example, the speech therapist or the social worker) of each IEP goal to go over our suggested changes and finalize the wording.

Remember, I'm a contract negotiator, and Alex is in audit…neither one of us signs anything without reading it, researching it, and correcting mistakes. The school district again pushed back and informed us that they wanted their lawyer present while we discussed our proposed changes with the whole team. They wouldn't allow us to work directly with the therapists responsible for each goal. *Um, okay. Fine by me.* I worked with lawyers every day and knew the school was overreacting and trying to intimidate us. Their scare tactics didn't work, and we got everything on paper that Max needed to succeed in class.

Max's IEP was finalized at the end of his first-grade year (this is **not** a quick process, even without added drama). Our next step was figuring out how to create a better team dynamic with his new second-grade teacher. The minute we found out who she was, I sent her an email introducing myself and Max, giving her an overview of his needs and the gist of the IEP. These plans are dense and use very formal language, and each teacher may have multiple sets to read each year. My goal was to give her a cheat sheet, so she and Max could start the year off on the right foot. (Little did I know this is actually a "best practice" within the Special Education community. You'll find a sample template called "New School Year Transition Guide" at *rebegoebel.com/bookresources*.)

Everything was going well in second grade. Max started behavior therapy, and we closely watched his progress, thinking we might need to add some medication to his treatment plan. Therapy helped with some of his ADHD challenges, like getting stuck on an idea or a particular way of doing things and not being flexible, or the struggles he had with starting a task he wasn't looking forward to doing, but his reading and writing skills weren't improving. We had just started the conversation with his doctor about what we were seeing at home and at school when life threw us two curveballs – one we saw coming and the other one caught us completely unaware.

By the end of October, we knew we would be moving the family from Chicago to St. Louis, Alex's hometown, where he had received a great job offer. We decided I would quit my corporate job, at least for a while, to get the family settled and to chase this crazy dream I had to be my own boss and a writer, not to mention being more hands-on with our boys, who were four and seven at the time.

Next up, we had to move the IEP we had basically **just** finalized, with a solid, supportive team in place, to a whole new state! Easy peasy, right? Actually, it was relatively smooth because I took all the lessons I'd learned the hard way in Chicago and started fresh in Missouri with a lot of experience under my belt.

I called the new school and asked about the process for transferring over an IEP. While the details of that process aren't important, the way I approached the new school is. I immediately started a positive and clear dialogue. I established myself as an active, informed member of the IEP team. I started and ended every interaction with genuine gratitude for the work they were doing on behalf of my family. I owned my part in leading and communicating with the team from day one.

We've had our ups and downs over the decade we've been in St. Louis. Some teams have been better than others, but as Max enters his senior year as I write this, I can thankfully say he's thriving.

3

AT LEAST THE SECOND TIME I HAD A LANTERN

But wait, Rebe, hold up. You said that there were two curveballs and that you have two kids with special needs? What about Henry? Where was he during all this? What's his story?

While, in hindsight, I can see that both of my children started showing signs of needing help around age two or three, our early experiences with Henry varied significantly. The team of teachers in several of his daycare classrooms was newer, lacking the wealth of experience needed to recognize the early signs of a child with potential special needs. Nor did any of them have strong communication skills with parents.

This led to being completely surprised during a routine parent-teacher conference when the director stepped in and began using words like aggression, explosions, tantrums, and refusal to comply with directions. To be honest, we really hadn't seen any of those behaviors at home. Henry is the youngest of a pack of four cousins – of course, he had to work twice as hard to keep up with them. He wasn't like Max had been, impulsive and struggling to keep his hands to himself. He was never climbing the walls with excess energy or demanding our attention constantly. In fact, he was a relatively easy toddler, and I reveled in how exceptional he was at entertaining himself for hours at a time. Because of these differences, it had never occurred to us that lighting might strike us twice and that both of our boys would have some sort of special needs.

After asking some of our standard questions (like, "help me understand how his behavior is different from what you see in his peers"), we didn't get answers that led us to believe his behavior was out of the ordinary for high-energy little boys. And to be honest? We were in the fight of our lives to get Max what he needed over at the elementary school. All our energy was consumed by the battle raging there, and we didn't take their concerns about Henry as seriously as we probably should have.

Fast forward through a year of relative silence from the daycare, and we pick the story back up right after we moved to St. Louis. He started a new preschool and was placed in a classroom with two highly skilled, veteran teachers. This is where the shit hit the fan, folks. Looking back, I believe there had probably been concerning behaviors present all along, but after our move turned Henry's world upside down, they really escalated.

Almost from day one, it was apparent he was in crisis. I don't use that word lightly. While I'd been concerned with Max (and righteously pissed at the school), I was terrified by what was happening with Henry. He'd have a meltdown right after drop off, and they would call me 30 minutes into the day asking me to come get him. He was striking out at teachers and peers routinely, creating a safety concern for everyone involved. At home, he started to hit me, his grandmother, and his brother.

We never knew what little thing would set him off, so everyone was walking around on eggshells, Max included. Henry would scream, rip things up, and flip over tables and chairs, destroying anything he could get his hands on for hours until he was finally exhausted. He would try to physically run away from any negative feelings, dashing away from me into the grocery store parking lot and trying multiple times to escape the school building. He needed to be monitored during every minute of the day when he was around others.

It didn't matter what we did to try to communicate with him or calm him down – if he was in the middle of a meltdown, he was unreachable. He was locked away inside the chaos of his own mind and world. I was losing my four-year-old and it felt like the world I'd just gotten back on solid ground with Max was crumbling underneath my feet.

As things continued to worsen for the family, it became my full-time job to break Henry free from the cycle he was stuck in and get him the help he desperately needed. If you're familiar at all with pediatric specialists, it will come as no surprise to you that there are horrible wait times to see any of them. Through some dogged determination on my part and a series of divine interventions, we were able to get appointments relatively quickly with a therapist and for a series of psychological evaluations through St. Louis County services.

Henry had just turned five and was still so young that the psychologist doing the evaluations could only give us a tentative diagnosis of ADHD. And yet that still didn't help us in the day-to-day storm we were stuck living in. He was being sent home from preschool three times a week, and the **only** reason we weren't asked to leave mid-year is that my mother-in-law had taught there for over 20 years. There was no way I could send him to any sort of summer camp, nor could I keep him at the preschool for another year and delay his kindergarten year. The preschool wouldn't have him back, and he was aging out of early childhood services.

We worked closely with the teachers and preschool (who truly were doing their absolute best for us) and decided it was best to place him in kindergarten in the public school district for the next year, where he could have access to the supports provided there. Through some serious collaboration efforts, the school district rushed through an Early Childhood IEP for him so he'd start school in the fall with some supports already in place. It was 100% a team effort.

I struggle to find the words for how hard those months were for me. I suspect you might know what I'm talking about already. Looking back, I remember a series of moments where my spirit was so empty, I was sure I wasn't strong enough to get through the next minute, the next hour, let alone the next week or month. I was terrified of what might be wrong with Henry and what it would mean for our family and his future. I was heartbroken watching him be consumed by these rages we couldn't pull him out of. We couldn't get through to him at all while one was happening. I was so mad that everything took so much time – scheduling visits with specialists for three to six months in the future? What the hell?! Didn't they realize I needed help immediately, not in 90 days?!?

I was exhausted. I was exhausted from keeping all the paperwork, appointments, and advice straight. I was exhausted from tiptoeing around Henry, impossibly trying to avoid a meltdown. I was exhausted from focusing completely on him and having to keep myself tightly in check during an episode. I was exhausted from locking myself in the bathroom so I could cry my eyes out for 10 minutes before going back to the task that had been interrupted over an hour ago, when it had all gone sideways on me. I was exhausted from having to physically restrain a child wild with emotions he clearly couldn't process.

I. Was. Exhausted.

Henry started kindergarten needing full-time support from a para-educator. He literally could not be unsupervised and still had frequent meltdowns. Thank God I had already established a good relationship with the school the year before with Max. I was there daily to find out how Henry's day had gone. I was still called by the school multiple times to come and help calm him down. He struck out at friends and teachers, resulting in several days of out-of-school suspensions, and when he tried to escape the school, his teachers had to restrain him and transport him back into a classroom. (Side note: All the staff are trained how to do these things, and they had my full knowledge and consent to do so. Communication is key.)

Our pediatrician prescribed one low-dose medication to help with the ADHD, but it just wasn't enough. He finally told us he'd done all he was comfortable with for a child so young. It was time to find a pediatric psychiatrist. I won't even go into how long one place said we'd have to wait to even get the opportunity to schedule an appointment (nine months) or if the guy we found who could see us in six weeks took any insurance (he didn't) or how much we paid out of pocket to see him (I'm just thankful we had the money in savings). I waited those six weeks stewing in a slurry of hope and anxiety, wondering if this doctor would finally offer us the keys needed to unlock my baby from the prison his mind had become, if he was going to be another dead-end or worse yet, tell us something life-shattering.

In the end, after a solid hour of explaining all the meltdowns and behaviors and our worries and fears, the psychiatrist had good news for us. Henry's ADHD was the root cause of it all...it was just manifesting very differently than we had seen with Max. We started playing around with medications, in addition to continuing therapy, and slowly, Henry started to emerge from the fog that had been preventing him from successfully navigating the world around him. After winter break that year, he was also diagnosed with Tourette's Syndrome, and we finally landed on a combination of medication and therapy that worked, and things started to improve for him. Years later, again with the benefit of hindsight and more experience with Henry, he was also unsurprisingly diagnosed with autism spectrum disorder.

Through it all, I was in constant contact with the school, employing all the skills and tactics I'll teach you here in this book. We didn't make a step outside the school without me informing his teachers, so we were all on the same page, keeping expectations and reactions consistent for Henry. I made a point to park and walk up to the front of the school at the end of every day so I could have a quick daily conversation with his teacher, and we met informally as a larger team once a month. Frequent, concise communication kept us all heading in the right direction.

By the spring of his kindergarten year, we were seeing huge strides and growth in Henry, and I felt like I could finally exhale a bit. I knew our family had just survived a huge test – one your family may just be starting. I swore I would use my skills and talents to share what I had learned with other families, lighting those lanterns along the way so you wouldn't feel as alone and confused as I had been.

This brings us back full circle to why I've spent years writing this book. Getting your child the services they need is complicated and slow at the best of times. At the worst, it's infuriating, seemingly inaccessible, and full of roadblocks. However, from my own experiences and from supporting and advising other parents, I am certain that students succeed when they are supported by three equally strong pillars — Parental Advocacy, General Education, and Special Education. All three must work in close collaboration and be equally responsible partners in providing the support and services a child needs to achieve their own version of success. Regardless of how much the school is or isn't doing to support your child, **you** cannot be a passive participant. You have to be involved and effective, too, and that requires taking care of yourself.

Through the rest of this book, I will light a few key lanterns to guide your footsteps on this path. Your family's path won't be exactly the same as mine, but these lanterns will still shine for you, providing you do the work between them. You wouldn't be here if you weren't ready to roll up your sleeves, so let's get to it.

PART II

SANITY-SAVERS YOU'RE GOING TO NEED

THERE'S A REASON THIS CHAPTER comes before the nitty-gritty details of the IEP process or how to do all the communicating, negotiating, and overall navigating the special education and special needs world. There's a reason why this is the first lantern, and I'm telling you, "Do not skip this part."

You are the foundation of your child's team. You are the bedrock of their support system and the critical lynchpin in helping them get the services they need. If you do not care for yourself, the quality of care your child receives will suffer. Period.

I also understand just how freaking hard it is to care for yourself – especially when your kiddos need **more** support than normal. I know how hard it is to find a babysitter you trust to give them their evening meds on time or deal with whatever behaviors come up. I know the sting of mom-guilt — your choices are always judged and wrong in someone's eyes, sometimes even in your own. And I know how overwhelming it can feel to even figure out what would actually help you feel better/healthier/rested/what-have-you.

Social media wants to peddle us a fluffy version of self-care, or honestly, one that is the opposite of supportive (I'm looking at you, doom-scrolling past your bedtime and wine). True, lasting self-care isn't found at the end of a bubble bath or a bar of chocolate. Burnout isn't fixed by a vacation. You have to address the systems you have in place, the behaviors that led you to this moment, and the expectations you have of yourself and your situation in order to achieve a shred of the feelings you're searching for.

The good news is that these changes can start with easy, wildly practical and effective practices that fit into the life you have. Nothing I share here will require an hour spent in silent meditation, buying any equipment or supplements, or radical lifestyle changes. It can be as simple as taking two deep breaths.

I'll never forget the moment I knew, without a doubt, that I needed something to help me out of the spiral of frustration, fear, and rage I felt myself slipping into. I had just wrestled Henry into the car during a meltdown that had begun inside Target. Mortified by the public spectacle, I abandoned my cart, dealt with his flailing, screaming, and hitting, and finally clipped him into his car seat. I stood outside the car, vibrating with my own out-of-control energy, and knew I was on the verge of a tantrum myself. I took two deep breaths and thought, "I've got to get myself under control, too. I guess, maybe I should learn how to meditate."

I managed to get myself home that day without losing it all over my child – something that would have made me feel even worse and certainly would NOT have helped my son in that moment. But it was a close call. We were both in tears the whole way home.

I don't think anyone other than someone else in this community can really understand the toll that caring for a child with special needs takes on a parent. Unless you've agonized over which treatment is the right one to try and then which one you can afford, you don't get it. Unless you've dealt with a "medical" meltdown driven by a tiny nervous system that's overstimulated vs. a regular meltdown, you don't get it. Unless you've stood in the parking lot, your own scream and tears bubbling up because you are soul-weary and just trying to f*cking survive the moment you're in…you don't get it.

Mama, I see you. I get it.

Those two deep breaths taken in the Target parking lot got me through that moment. But what I found when I went to research meditation classes and techniques was so impractical that all I could do was shake my head. "Give us six months and an hour a day, and you'll find bliss," they promised. "All you need is $10,000 and complete silence during an hour a day, and you'll unlock the secrets of your mind!"

Ha! Yeah, right. An hour of silence was a myth, a freaking unicorn, barely to be found *once* during those six months, let alone daily. I needed practical, brutally efficient practices and tools that worked in the chaos of raising two neurodivergent kids and caring for my own aging parents. I needed meditation to work **in the moments** I needed it the most – when I was worn out, hungry, and when my own nervous system was overstimulated and about to give out on me.

So I did what I always do, I dove into research mode. Then I started experimenting and playing with meditation, mindfulness, breathwork, and somatic practices. Throughout it all, I was focused on a few key questions: How could I make it simpler? How could I make it faster? What's the minimum I can do to get the effect I'm looking for? And how can I make this work in the schedule and life I have right now?

Depending on where you're at in your journey, you may have already realized that you're running a marathon now. I wish I could tell you that IEPs are one-and-done. I wish I could tell you that what is working for your child at age five will still work when they are fifteen. I wish I could tell you a lot of things, Mama. But I wouldn't be doing my job here if I lied to you like that.

What I **can** tell you is that putting yourself last is absolutely a bad idea. Sure, there will be moments of crisis when your needs are less important than those of your child(ren). But I promise you will feel steadier, more confident, and more capable as a person, parent, and advocate for your child if you carve out intentional moments to care for yourself and move out of survival mode.

Perhaps you've already heard the "Welcome to Holland" metaphor written by Emily Perl Kingsley. In it, she compares her experience of having a child with special needs to preparing for a long-awaited trip to Italy, boarding the plane, and then, upon landing, discovering she is in Holland instead and must stay there. While there are some valid criticisms of her original writing, I think it's a solid starting point for acknowledging and exploring a myriad of very real emotions and thoughts parents experience throughout their experience.

I want to explore these thoughts with you here for a few reasons. First, if you continually deny your feelings, they will eventually get so pressurized you'll erupt with them, potentially causing harm to yourself and those around you. Second, in today's social media-driven cancel-culture, it can be really hard to find a space where others are talking about how hard this journey is without at least feeling attacked and judged as a terrible parent. And third, I want you to know that these feelings are normal and completely appropriate responses to being thrown a giant curveball. Having the skills to work through them as they come up is key to getting to the point where you can move forward with a clear mind.

When you first realize your child's path might be different from the one you imagined, it's normal to feel some grief and denial. It's hard to admit that your child may experience life-long challenges, and even harder to stop from asking the Universe, "why my kid"? In the search for answers, it's easy to slip into a blame and shame spiral, but I want you to hear me on this: you are not at fault, nor does assigning blame to anyone—including yourself—actually help your child get what they need today.

Depending on your community and the individuals in your family, you may feel judged by them, too. Or they may be stuck in their own denial, refusing to believe anything is wrong. This puts you in a terrible position of either needing to convince them of what you and your child are going through or questioning yourself and what experts/medical providers are telling you. Maybe you just haven't parented your child the right way. Maybe you're just a bad parent. You should have been stricter with your child, not let them eat anything artificial, not used a pacifier, etc.

You may find that after the initial wave of grief and confusion passes, anger and frustration come for a visit. It is absolutely maddening to get the help you need, to first just figure out what's going on with your child, and then to get the support you need for them. The wait times to see specialists can be nearly a year long, and that's assuming you're lucky enough to have one in your area. The financial toll of private-pay providers, added to the nightmare of premiums, deductibles, and everything else that comes with the American medical insurance system, is enough to break you.

And after a while, the overwhelm hits and exhaustion sets in. Because life just keeps life-ing, right? You've got aging parents, other children, work, a house with a broken faucet, a mountain of laundry, and, and, and. Your nervous system is shot from being on constant high alert.

Even 15 years into my journey, as my child's teenaged angst is spiced with a liberal dash of autism, I wish it were easier. I get so tired. I don't have all the answers. With teens, I can't really even fight their battles anymore. I find it difficult not to compare myself and my high-school experience (a neurotypical, driven oldest daughter who excelled in school and loves learning) to my children, who, even with IEPs and outside therapy, are struggling with increased expectations. I worry they don't understand how the choices they make in high school are shaping the options they will have later. I worry about their mental health. As issues come up, I struggle to decipher if they need better tools to cope or if they're just being a-holes, because how I respond to those two scenarios would be wildly different. I worry about their futures. I worry. So much.

All that to say, you're not alone, no matter what you're feeling. And I have both good and bad news. The bad news is that I don't have all the answers for your specific situation. I can't tell you why you, why your kid, why the system is so broken, or why support is so hard to get. I can't tell you how to best parent your child. I can't even promise that, even if you use every tool, tip, and trick in this book, you will get everything you need from a resource-constrained educational system. Sorry, babe. I wish I could.

However, the good news is that I can help you feel a little less alone, a lot smarter, and a whole lot steadier as you travel this path. In this section, you're going to learn how to deal with the emotions as they come and how to get your nervous system out of a trauma-response and into a state that supports you. You are your own foundation, and as such, you are the only one capable of and responsible for how steady it is.

Your personal history, including your cultural upbringing and life experiences, will play a large factor in determining how you initially respond when the going gets rough. We all have trauma in our lives. Trauma is an emotional, physical, and mental response to an experience or series of experiences that you didn't feel like you had the tools needed to deal with during and after an event in your life. It is highly subjective what any person experiences as trauma. It could be as simple as getting lost from your caregivers as a child to experiencing long-term neglect and abuse. I mention these moments from your past because when we get triggered or dysregulated today, it is because something happening **now** reminds our body and subconscious of what happened **then**, bringing it all rushing back to the surface. It doesn't matter that you're no longer five years old and have a whole different set of capabilities and resources to resolve issues today – your brain jumps right back to the first time you felt the way you do right now.

You will get triggered as you walk this path. Every single one of us does. Period. You will freeze when you don't know what to do. You will want to lash out or fight when the school denies your request for something. You will want to run away and pretend like nothing is wrong. These are all normal responses to a very stressful situation where you have a ton of very valid concerns about your child and feel like the other side holds all the power. You. Will. Get. Triggered.

The point of doing this work is not to make you trigger-proof. Anyone who tells you that they never get upset, hurt, or frustrated is in denial and is just at the opposite end of the spectrum of the person who overreacts to everything. And we know through emerging studies around trauma and epigenetics that when emotions aren't dealt with, what's repressed or is allowed to fester will eventually express itself **physically** through illness, autoimmune disease, and burnout.

In many online circles, and maybe sadly even in your discussions with well-meaning but misinformed friends and professionals, you may be told the goal for **both you and your child** is to "regulate your nervous system." It is physically impossible for you to be "regulated" all the time, so this goal sets you up for immediate failure. I propose you work towards a different goal: learn how to truly take care of yourself and build enough resilience so that you can *navigate* your nervous system. You want to know that when shit goes sideways, because it will, that you have the tools to navigate your natural response and return to your own sense of equilibrium.

So we know you're going to get triggered – by your child, your partner, the dipshit who can't follow the carpool line rules, or during a meeting with the school. What can you do about it? What can you do **before** your trauma-response of fight/flight/freeze kicks in to be an effective navigator of your nervous system?

As it turns out, quite a bit! This is where we get into the meat and potatoes of self-care. These are the things I want you to start adding to your daily – yes, daily – routine to build up some resilience in your nervous system.

Think of your nervous system as a bank account— whenever you can, your goal should be to deposit energy and care to add to your balance.

This way, when a rough day or rough season comes along, you have a cushion to support the withdrawals you'll need to make.

I'm going to teach you a handful of simple practices that will help you understand, navigate, and support not only **your** nervous system, but many can be used with your child as well. They also come with a whopper of a permission slip — You are hereby given express permission to take only what works for you and ignore the rest. You are given permission to make these practices **even** simpler. You are given permission to make them your own. You are given permission to pick a different one every day and make it playful and fun. You are given permission to include your kids and your partner.

You are given permission to carve out a few minutes just for yourself. Every. Single. Day.

As we go, I will note where I have additional resources that expand on these tools and techniques and how to find them. There are also some free meditations specifically for you available on my website: *rebe-goebel.com/bookresources*.

4

ESTABLISH YOUR FOUNDATION

FIRST AND FOREMOST, you've got to make sure your basic physical needs are met. People like to joke about being "hangry," but we've all experienced it. Hunger, dehydration, and exhaustion all impact how we show up in our lives. These physical needs impact your capacity to handle everything in your life, from snagging your pocket on the drawer handle to navigating life-changing discussions.

In Dr. Ellen Vora's book, *The Anatomy of Anxiety*, this is exactly where she has her patients start, because as it turns out, the feelings we associate with anxiety are often actually the body's way of getting our attention when something is off **physically**. "True" anxiety does exist, but she has found that for a large number of people, resolving underlying health issues and cleaning up their habits makes a huge difference in their mental health.

So, go back to the basics. Are you getting enough sleep? Are you fueling your body with nutrient-rich food? Do you have a leaky gut or high levels of inflammation in your body? Are you drinking too much caffeine or alcohol? Eating late at night? I promise you, I know how annoying I sound right now. I didn't want to make most of these changes either, but damn if it doesn't make a huge difference. It's boring, basic, and not a quick fix, but there's a reason everyone and their cousin shouts about sleep and nutrition.

Making changes in your lifestyle is hard, but there are some research-backed ways to make adopting a new habit easier. One, focus first on **adding beneficial habits**, rather than eliminating the less supportive ones. For example, you might want to drink more water and less alcohol. Start by keeping your wine intake the same, but adding a glass of water before each glass of wine. You may find you have one less glass of wine because your stomach is full and you no longer want it. If you're trying to get more sleep, change your bedtime slowly, shifting it 15 minutes at a time.

The next thing you can do to support habit change is to **pair the new habit with an existing one**. I love taking the 3-5 minutes while my tea kettle brews in the morning to put my hand on my heart, take some deep, centering breaths, and check in with how I'm feeling and what I need for the day. I also tell my clients to pair taking two deep breaths with every stop sign or stop light they come across during their commute or errands. The key here is to pair something you do every single day – walking the dog, brewing your coffee, brushing your teeth –with the new habit you want to add. Then the new habit just becomes one more step of an already established routine, making it that much easier to keep it going.

The last thing that really helps with adopting a new habit is to **set the bar really low** at first. I mean, really low. You want to start exercising? Your goal is simply to put on your exercise clothes every day and move your body for 5 minutes. Maybe you don't even need to change your clothes. It could be dancing to your favorite song in your pjs while your coffee or tea brews. It could be stretching for a few minutes before you even get out of bed. It could be walking to the end of your street and back. But that's where you can start.

5

YOU ARE MORE THAN JUST A BODY

Now, once you've started working on your body's physical needs, let's talk about simple and effective ways you can care for your mind-body connection – your nervous system. Contrary to popular belief, I don't recommend you start with meditation. Depending on the state of your system and your own spot on the neuro-spicy spectrum, sitting down in a quiet space and trying to clear your mind might feel really awful and not supportive of your goals. In the following section, I'm going to teach you a couple of different exercises that are easy to do, take less than five minutes if you're in a rush, and still produce massive results when done even semi-consistently.

As human beings, we get stuck in the trap of overcomplicating things to the point that they're no longer supportive. A daily mindfulness practice is the perfect example. It can be done in moments, at any time of day, but we get tied up in knots thinking we need 20-30 minutes, in a perfectly clean house, in a Pinterest-worthy, Zen space, with absolute silence, and all while wearing matching loungewear. Bah.

Listen, I love a juicy, hours-long self-care splurge as much as the next exhausted mama. But for my daily practices – the ones that keep me feeling centered and my energy replenished while I'm doing the earthy, gritty work of caring for my family – I'm not interested in anything that even remotely approaches *aesthetic.* My practice rarely looks the same from day to day, but it is always practical, supportive, and effective.

One last note before I start teaching you any of these practices _ if you've been stuck in a heightened, stressed state, even taking two deep breaths can make your body feel uncomfortable. Your system is primed to see everything in your environment as a threat and may respond accordingly. As you meditate, and especially if you do any sort of sustained breathwork practice, know that it is normal and natural for your heart rate to fluctuate, for you to feel tingling in your extremities or around your mouth, or for your muscles to twitch. These practices are **designed** to change how your body, and therefore mind, feels, and your body may have an autonomic response to changes in your breathing pattern. In most cases, this is normal and expected, and should return to your baseline quickly after your practice ends.

This is also where I give you a huge warning — if you are pregnant, have any cardiac issues, brain injury, issues with your retinas or the pressure in your eyes, or severe, untreated mental illness, you **absolutely should not** do any intense breathing exercises without first consulting with a medical professional.

All of the practices I detail here are gentle and should be safe for anyone to participate in, but if you fall into any of the categories above, please take a moment to consult someone on your medical team. When in doubt, err on the side of caution and remove any breathing cues I've included, focusing instead on maintaining a slow, natural breathing pattern and treating the practice as a meditation or visualization. You will still gain benefits from doing so.

Micro-Meditation

I've already mentioned the first practice that I want you to add to your toolkit - taking two deep breaths. In fact, I'd like you to do so here in just a second. This first time, take a moment to check in with your body and mind. What's one word that you could use to describe your state? Tense? Tired? Overwhelmed? How are you breathing right now?

Okay, now roll your shoulders back and down and take a deep breath in through your nose, down into your belly. Without holding your breath at all, gently breathe out through your mouth. Do it one more time, in through your nose and out through your mouth.

Notice how you feel now. Did you feel your shoulders lose some tension? Did your heart rate and energy slow down, so now you feel a tiny bit more centered? Do you feel just a smidge better – like if you did this again in the middle of your kiddo's meltdown or a tense moment with your spouse, you might be more intentional with your next words and actions? Yes? Excellent! Now pair these two deep breaths with something you do all the time – my favorites are every time you're at a stop sign/light, but if you work from home and don't run carpool anymore, do it every time you go to the bathroom. Seriously. Put down your phone for the first 5-10 seconds and breathe.

That's it. That's as complicated as it needs to be. Two deep breaths taken with intention, taken again and again, every single day. Over time, the cumulative benefits of just this one practice will have a dramatic impact on your ability to stay present and aligned with who you want to be and how you want to respond in the hard moments – the moments you need it the most.

Mindfulness is More Than Sitting Still

Another way you can add to your personal energy bank is to weave mindfulness into your other daily activities. Check in with yourself and see what tasks or chores you enjoy doing or that allow you to zone out – where your mind quiets and clarity can come through. For me, it's in the shower. For my husband, it's while he's out in our yard. I even have a friend who finds peace in the grocery store. Whatever it is for you, capitalize on that and make every part of that activity intentional. If I'm taking a walk, I might skip music altogether to give my mind space to wander and wonder, or I might take the first 20 minutes to listen to a playlist with songs that bring my spirit back into alignment before switching to a podcast or audiobook.

If you want to try your hand at stillness or meditation, I highly recommend either starting small by listening to one song that brings you peace or adding structure to your meditation practice. If you choose to listen to a song, your goal for the duration of that song is to close your eyes and simply breathe while you focus on the song. As you notice thoughts popping up (which they will, because your brain is designed to think), the practice is to gently, **gently**, bring your attention back to the song and let the thoughts go.

If you want to try a structured meditation, set aside 5-10 minutes and head to my website, where I have a video that walks you through the four parts of this practice. As an overview, though, you're going to settle in and take two deep breaths while you gently close your eyes. First, start by thinking of something you're truly grateful for and give thanks to Source/the Universe/God/the divine entity of your choice. This isn't about creating a long list. Here, I want you to allow yourself to sink into the energy of gratitude for one thing. Second, you will choose one person, event, region of the world, etc., to send a good or healing thought to. This is very similar to "lifting someone up in prayer," but even if you're not the praying type, you can mentally send your best wishes to someone who is going through it. And yes, you can absolutely lift yourself up here. That's allowed.

For your third step, you're going to scan your body and mind, checking in with yourself to see what **you** need to give yourself today. Do you need to rest? Do you need to connect with others? Do you need a boost of energy to get things done? Do you need to say no to a pending commitment? Allow whatever pops into your mind first to be your choice. Don't judge it, don't talk yourself out of it, don't ignore it. It may not make sense to your logical mind. During meditation, you are in much closer alignment with your intuition and higher self – trust the whispers that come through.

And finally, you're going to allow yourself to settle into a few moments of silence. Focus on your breath moving in through your nose and out through your mouth. You can make this part as short or as long as you like. The important thing is that you give yourself time to just be. I like to say that prayer is when we ask the Universe our questions, but meditation is when we shut up and listen for the answers. If you're never still and quiet, you've made no space for support, clarity, and peace to arrive. When you're ready, take two last deep breaths and roll out your wrists and shoulders, bringing some gentle movement back into your body before opening your eyes. Notice how you feel and remember what your body/higher-self told you that you need for today. You're now centered and better equipped to handle anything your day brings.

Energy Shielding

As with all these tools and techniques I discuss in this section, please remember you are free to take what works for **you** and leave the rest. This happens to be my second most used practice and one you can do daily, but is especially helpful to do just before a tense or stressful situation.

One last practice I want to share with you here dives deeper into energy work. Energy shielding is the process of taking a moment to check in with yourself and then setting the intention that no matter what other energies you run into, they don't get to attach to your energy without your permission.

The best way I can think to explain this is to ask you to imagine a big family gathering, like Thanksgiving. If your family is like mine, even if you generally all like each other, there's always *something* going on. Someone is pissed because they couldn't wear sweatpants, Aunt Sally is stressed because her turkey turned out bone dry, your sister-in-law is the worst gossip, and Uncle Bob is, well, who he is. Everyone is just hoping he doesn't bring up some whackadoodle conspiracy theory. We all have an Uncle Bob.

Ugh. It's a fictional family at a fictional dinner, and you can still probably **feel** the energy of that gathering. We've all walked into a meeting, place, or event and felt that the energy was off. If you're not shielded, it's so easy for the energy or mood of those around you to negatively impact you. As we are all creatures of energy, and take our cues both consciously and subconsciously from those around us, this is a predictable outcome of coming into contact with others, from your partner to those you just brush up against in a crowded restaurant. The more sensitive you are and the more your own childhood survival required you to be aware of the moods and energy of those around you, the more critical this practice will be for you. (Ahem. Ask me how I know.)

The practice of energy shielding allows you to form a protective barrier between your energy and the vibes you may have to wade through, while not closing you off entirely. You don't want to block yourself off from the good stuff – the love and support others offer you – just the unwelcome energy drain of all the other nonsense. I use this practice before every IEP meeting, networking event, and social gathering.

The actual practice of energy shielding is one part meditation, one part visualization, and one part "energy work," but please don't let that term scare you off from trying this technique. You work with your energy every day when you drink an extra soda for a pick-me-up, when you go to bed early because you're extra tired, and when you notice something is wrong before your child ever says that their tummy hurts. I promise you can do this!

So, going back to our fictional Thanksgiving dinner, how should you shield your energy before you even get there? As with all the practices I've laid out for you, you can do this on the fly, as you're walking up the sidewalk, or you can set aside as much time as you would like to in order to make it into a juicy self-care moment.

Assuming you've got 5-10 minutes, start by finding a quiet space and either sitting or lying down. Close your eyes and take a few deep, centering breaths, pulling the air in through your nose and down into your belly. Hold your breath for a moment if you'd like to, and then allow that breath to release through your mouth. Allow yourself to make your exhale noisy, maybe even wiggling your jaw back and forth a bit to release any tension stored there.

Once you're settled, I invite you to bring your attention to your heart space and imagine a small orb of light centered right there in your heart. Notice how it shimmers, and you can see through it, but it's sturdy and strong. As you keep breathing and focusing on this orb, notice how it begins to grow. Slowly, it expands out from your heart, filling your whole torso, and growing until you are fully enveloped inside this bubble of light.

Delighted, you examine the bubble more closely. Noticing how it flexes when you press your hand to the inside, how the air flows freely, passing right through it, and how love and light also move through the surface, reaching you easily. Perhaps you notice how safe you feel, surrounded by this pure energy. Perhaps you feel grounded, like you're standing on an unshakeable foundation. Now, notice how any negativity around you might come close, but bounces right off your protective shield, repelled and returned to its source.

Take as long as you like here, resting in this pool of protection. When you're ready, set an intention for your energy and mind for the rest of the day. It might be something like, "My energy is mine. Your energy is yours." Or, "I am in control of how I respond to people's energy and comments. They don't have the power to provoke me out of alignment." Or simply, "I am grounded. I am protected. I am safe."

As you set this intention, imagine your bubble of light getting even stronger as it shrinks down to hover just millimeters above your skin, like invisible armor.

As you get ready to close out your practice, I invite you to bring up a hand and place it on your heart. Draw in two more deep breaths and open your eyes. Your energy is now protected. Your only job is to remember that you are shielded as you go about your day.

If you find yourself with less than 5 minutes, you can strip this practice down to the quick-and-dirty basics. While taking a few deep breaths, jump right to envisioning yourself surrounded by your bubble of light. Repeat "My energy is mine. Your energy is yours." 2-3 times, take one last deep breath, and you're done.

Remember, self-care is a flexible tool you can bend to fit the situation you're in—not a rigid practice that must be followed exactly. You can't screw this up!

6

WHAT TO DO IN THE MOMENT YOU GET TRIGGERED

Okay, you've found a couple of techniques and practices that work for you and your schedule, and you're going about your day, feeling good, then BAM! Something happens. You get a call from the school, your kiddo has a total meltdown in public, the pipe breaks under your cabinet, whatever it might be, and now you're in the thick of it. You notice your breathing has gotten shallow, adrenaline dumps into your system, and you know you're in the middle of a trauma response – fight, flight, or freeze. Now what do you do?

Here's the thing about getting triggered – your body can't tell the difference between getting a shitty text from your sister and the life-threatening attack of a lion. For millennia, most danger was life-threatening, so our nervous systems evolved to respond in kind – by funneling blood flow and energy away from your brain and shutting down digestion and sending the resources into your arms and legs so you can run away or fight.

Today, we still respond like that, but our modern issues, 1) don't usually require that level of response, and 2) happen way more frequently than our nervous systems have evolved to handle. Every day, we're bombarded by bad news from around the world and by thousands of emails, texts, and alerts, all of which can trigger our nervous systems. You may not even be conscious that your system has slipped into a constant state of high-alert. This is what lands us in chronic levels of stress. If you can, focus on giving yourself grace. **You are going to get triggered** because life is overwhelming and your system is hardwired for certain responses. You may lash out or dissociate for a moment, and that's okay. These are **normal** initial responses.

Once you realize that your system has been activated, though, the first thing you're going to do is the micro-meditation: two deep breaths, in through the nose and out through the mouth, paying extra attention to making the exhales longer than the inhales. This is the first tool in your repertoire because it's so damn easy, **and** you can do it unobtrusively. I've literally done this in the middle of a meeting and no one was the wiser. The longer exhales signal to your body that you're safe, allowing your primitive brain to slow down and your thinking brain to come back online.

When the shit is really hitting the fan, two deep breaths might be all you have time for, and sometimes it may be all you need to reset your nervous system. You can also try focusing on something physical in your environment to pull your focus outside of your mind. You can either notice something around you or pick up something small to hold in your hand, bringing all your attention to its texture, color, weight, etc.

If you are able, regardless of what's going on, sit down on the ground. I don't care if it's the floor in the grocery store aisle; the act of sitting down sends signals to your brain that you're okay, and you can borrow the earth's energy and stability when you are, quite literally, grounded. Bonus points if you can step outside and get your butt, feet, and hands into the grass.

If you're really starting to spiral and have the ability to do so, give yourself a time-out and step away from the situation. I found that even when the kids were little, they understood what I was doing and why when I told them, "I need a minute or two in my room. I'll be right back." If your child gets overstimulated easily and needs breaks themselves, this is a great way to model the behavior you are trying to teach them and use similar language. Depending on their age, you could say some version of, "You know how sometimes the world is just too loud and busy for your brain? And then you need a minute in a quieter spot with your fidget or lovey to feel good again? I'm feeling that way right now. It's not anything you've done, baby, I just need to give my brain what I know it needs right now."

Obviously, please make sure that small children remain appropriately supervised, but don't feel guilty for needing to step away when your system has hit overdrive. When you put yourself in time-out, though, what you're **not** going to do is pick up your phone to scroll. During your time-out, you are going to do two things. First, you're going to lie down with your butt against the wall and stretch your legs up the wall, so you look like an "L." This gentle inversion gets your legs above your heart, encouraging blood flow to return to your core and brain. Remember how you learned that trauma responses pull your blood out to your extremities? This reverses that flow, using gravity to help, all of which lets your body know that the lion-level threat response is no longer necessary.

Now, while your legs are up in the air, I want you to do at least one round of this breathing exercise before you let yourself out of mommy-jail: breathe deeply and slowly, counting your inhales and exhales until you hit twenty. Yep, that's it. Inhale through your nose – one. Exhale through your mouth – two. Inhale – three. And so on, until you hit twenty.

Even if you're not in a spot where you can get your legs up a wall (or your mobility prevents you from doing so), you can keep this "Count to 20" exercise in your hip pocket. Listen, I know it sounds stupidly simple. That's the point. It has to be that simple to work when you're overwhelmed and your thinking-brain has gone offline. I used this technique during a 45-minute MRI on my brain to stave off a full-blown claustrophobia-induced panic attack. I hate small spaces and wasn't sure I'd be able to handle having my head strapped down and being shoved into a loud AF tube when I couldn't have headphones, because it was an MRI of my brain. But I did it.

You might lose track of your count, and that's totally normal – expected even. Just stay there and start your count over again. Inhale – one… Once your energy has settled again, head back out and do what needs to be done to address the situation.

7

HOW TO SUPPORT YOURSELF AFTER YOU GET TRIGGERED

While the techniques I just shared are wonderful for helping you when you're triggered, it's really important to take a few moments afterward to fully process your response to whatever happened. Otherwise, one thing rolls right on to the next, the hits keep on coming, and you stay in that triggered state. If you don't guide your nervous system back to neutral, you really haven't actually processed the energy and emotions that came up for you.

Like I've said before, yes, I love having a lot of time to go through this process. That's the ideal and the dream. If you can carve that time out, I love that for you. Truly. But if your loved one just had a medical emergency and you've only got a snippet of time before you're headed back to the hospital, here are the short and effective ways for you to let your body's trauma response run through its complete cycle and return to your baseline.

Shake It Off

Have you ever had a near miss where you just barely escaped an accident, and afterwards, your whole body starts to shake? Most of us criticize this response, thinking it is a sign of weakness or not being able to handle the situation, and we try to stop the shaking and "calm down" as soon as possible. As it turns out, that shaking is the way our body was designed to purge that dump of adrenaline we needed to stay safe. Animals do this all the time, but **they** don't have egos that get in the way and tell them they're being stupid. They just let themselves run around and shake until their body naturally stops.

So, the first thing I want you to do, even if your body didn't naturally start shaking, is to channel your inner Taylor Swift and shake it off. You can put on music if you'd like, but you're going to allow yourself to shake/vibrate/wiggle for a minimum of two minutes straight. You're going to shake your hands, your arms, your legs, your booty, and your head. You're going to let your body make whatever shape it wants and make your movements as big or as little as you'd like. Don't worry about what it looks like and let it be weird. This allows your body to burn off the last little bits of cortisol and adrenaline and complete the stress cycle before it gets stored into your cells.

After you've allowed your body to shake, you can check in with yourself to see what other practices might feel supportive this time. I've provided a few options here, but remember to check in with yourself first and foremost and trust whatever wisdom comes through for you.

Butterfly Taps

If your body needs more grounding or regulation, and you've already tried sitting on the ground with your legs up a wall, you can try resyncing the two sides of your brain by doing some gentle bilateral stimulation. To do this, give yourself a hug, placing your right hand on your left shoulder and your left hand on your right shoulder. Start with giving yourself an actual hug and then slowly start to tap yourself on the shoulder, one side at a time, remembering to breathe nice and gently. Keep doing this for a minimum of two minutes, but really, you can keep doing it until you feel yourself starting to relax.

Post-trauma processing sometimes looks and sounds like just giving yourself the permission to name exactly what you're feeling without judging yourself for it. When my mom had a heart attack, a mere six months after the stroke that took away her independence and made me her primary caretaker, I remember driving back to the hospital the next day. I just allowed myself to say everything I was feeling out loud to the empty car before I got there. I admitted I was pissed, and tired, and sad, and scared, and annoyed, and all the other emotions rioting in my head and heart. Not only did this allow me to honor how I was feeling and process what had happened the day prior, but it also gave me a chance to clear my head and heart before going in to see her. I was able to walk into her hospital room and give her the dignity, attention, and care she deserved without the cloud of my feelings and resentment hanging over me.

Get It Out of Your Head

Another thing that really helps with sorting through post-trigger emotions is to journal. The act of getting your thoughts out of your head and onto paper, literally of holding a pen in your hand and making marks, is transformative in a truly alchemical way. Have you ever seen someone meditating with the tip of their first finger and thumb connecting to form a circle? Now look at how you hold a pen. It's a very similar position, isn't it? Writing can connect us to ourselves, the divine/Source/God, and others. Writing out your thoughts clears the air and allows you to gain some perspective and clarity. Through journaling, you may even get to the point where you realize that you are the thinker of your thoughts – **you** are bigger than your thoughts. You, as an entity, have a brain, and your brain's job is to think. **You** are more than your brain and certainly more than your thoughts. Writing them out frees up mental space for creativity and for solutions to arise once the clutter is gone.

I find journaling to be helpful both before and after an IEP meeting. Beforehand, I will sit down and brain dump all my thoughts, from what I want to celebrate about my child to the concerns and questions I need to bring up. This process helps me organize everything rattling around in my head so I can communicate effectively during the meeting. It also lets me anticipate and deal with my feelings before I'm in front of others and need to have my head on straight. After an IEP meeting, journaling allows you to reflect on what happened, how you felt, and process any triggers that came up for you.

Even if you've tried journaling in the past and it didn't take, let me gently encourage you to give it another shot, perhaps in a way you've never approached it before. Many of us grew up with the idea that journaling is a "Dear Diary," sort of activity where we recount what happened during the day, or we complain about someone/something, or maybe like it's a place to tell a cohesive story. There are, of course, times when that can be very helpful, but I'd like to suggest a couple of different approaches.

The first option for you to consider is to journal with zero intention of keeping what you write. I love a fancy, aesthetically pleasing journal, but some things need to be purged out of your heart and mind onto paper and then gotten rid of safely. Feel free to start your journaling practice in one of your kids' leftover spiral notebooks. Write whatever it is you need to say and then rip it out of the notebook and shred, burn (SAFELY), or bury the pages to fully exorcize those thoughts.

Another option is to simply set a timer for 15-20 minutes and allow yourself to dump, and I mean dump, every thought in your head out onto paper. You're not going to go back and read it, you're never going to show what you wrote to anyone else, and you're not going to worry about anything but putting words down on paper for the allotted time. All of it. You're going to allow this to be messy. You're not going to worry about following a cohesive storyline. You're going to brain dump. It could be a list of things you're worried about. It might be recounting your dream from the night before. It may be a rant about *gestures broadly at the world in frustration.* The point is to have a catharsis, a complete release of your emotions, tensions, and thoughts, so you get it all out of your system. Then, once your head and heart are clear, you can return to your daily life with all of its challenges, feeling like you're on a bit more stable ground.

Some of my clients like to work from some prompts instead of a blank sheet of paper. If you get stuck feeling like you have no idea where to start and what to write, answering a question or two can get the juices flowing. You can do a quick search on Pinterest, Google, or AI (if that's your thing) for "journaling prompts for [insert your topic here]" and you'll get tons of suggestions. I've also included some prompts for you here. My one caveat here is that you don't use your journaling time to search for prompts. It can be so easy to spend the 20 minutes you were supposed to be writing farting around on the internet instead. Don't do that! Instead, find your prompts while you're sitting on the couch watching Gilmore Girls for the tenth time, so they're ready to go when you need them.

My last suggestion, if, for whatever reason, putting pen to paper doesn't work for you, is to try either a video or voice note journal. Open the right app on your phone and just ramble or follow the "journaling" prompts below in verbal form. Create a folder to keep all your entries together or delete them as you go. Play around with what works for you. Keep experimenting until you land on something that feels supportive. Remember — you have permission to do it any way you want!

Journaling/Reflection Prompts and Exercises

- Free-writing exercise: Set a timer for ten minutes and just write. Allow yourself to fully express your grief, anger, or confusion. The goal is to get all your thoughts and feelings out onto paper. Unlike most journaling exercises, this one isn't about saving your thoughts to go over again later. When you're done, safely destroy the papers, either by ripping them up, burying them, or (again, safely!) burning them.
- Where do you feel like you need more support? Brainstorm ways that would make you feel more supported.
- Which of the daily self-care habits do you want to implement immediately?
- Which one do you feel the most resistance to trying? Why do you think this resistance is popping up? Can you commit to trying it at least once, just as an experiment?
- Where do you feel like you need more knowledge? Brainstorm places you could learn what you need to know.

Cord-Cutting

The final technique I recommend for processing a stressful event is more energetic in nature. Think of a charged or uncomfortable situation or conversation you've had in the past. It could be a long time ago or last week; it doesn't really matter. Have you found yourself going over and over it since it happened? As I'm asking you to remember what happened, can you still feel the same emotions you did while it was happening? Even if the feeling has changed since then, do you still feel like there's an emotional charge around it? Like it still has its hooks in you? If so, you've got what's called an energetic cord tying you and your energy back to the past. I'm going to teach you how to cut that sucker so it stops siphoning off your energy.

Before we dive into the how, let's dive into a bit more about cord-cutting as a practice. Cord-cutting is a visualization/meditation where you symbolically cut any energetic connections that you feel don't serve your best interests. Cord-cutting works so well because your subconscious mind actually can't process time. For your subconscious, every time you remember an event, it reacts and triggers physical reactions as if the event is happening again right this very second. Visualizing yourself removing or cutting any connection you might still feel to something that happened in the past can help your brain finally get the message that it is done, and you can move on.

Cord-cutting can be a practice that takes 30 seconds or 30 minutes, so you can flex it to be down and dirty in the moment, or you can light a candle and make a juicy self-care session out of it. You can cut cords with events or people, including loved ones. It's important to note that cutting a cord with someone does not mean you're cutting them out of your life. You're simply removing their unapproved, and perhaps unhealthy, ongoing access to your energy.

You may find that you want to remove the energetic tie between yourself and a family member who never has nice things to say about your child or your parenting (see more in Chapter 25 "When Family or Those Close to You Aren't Supportive"). You might still be ruminating about who said what, or what you wish you had said, during the last IEP meeting, and want to let it go. As the eldest daughter, I've found that I have taken on way more responsibility for others and their happiness than is healthy for me. I have no ill will towards them, and they never overtly asked me to do it, but somewhere along the way, I did. Cutting those cords energetically, along with setting some boundaries, has been key to reclaiming that energy for myself while staying in a loving, close relationship with them.

When you are ready to try cord-cutting for the first time, make sure you've got 5-10 minutes where you will be uninterrupted and can get comfortable. After I go through the practice in detail, I'll share the quick and dirty version as well. For me, this practice feels better in a sitting or even standing position, but you should experiment to see which you prefer: sitting, standing, or lying down.

Close your eyes and take a few deep cleansing breaths, slowly bringing all your attention to the air moving in through your nose, filling your chest and belly, and then flowing back out either through your mouth or your nose. As you settle here, begin to bring your attention to your body, starting with a quick scan, bringing your awareness to your mind and just allowing yourself to notice what's present here. Acknowledging any thoughts, but passing no judgement and adding no meaning to anything you find. With your next inhale, follow that breath in through your nose and down into your chest, bringing your awareness here, allowing it to rest quietly, and just observe any physical sensations, noticing any tension or tightness in your shoulders. Perhaps you find your body wants to move a little bit here, rolling your shoulders down and back, opening across your chest, making more space for your heart and becoming gently aware of any emotions or feelings that might be present. One more time, I'm going to ask you to shift your awareness down deeper into your belly, towards your hips, checking in on any physical sensations that might be present here.

I invite you to imagine that you take a step outside of your body and look back at yourself. As you scan yourself, notice where you might have a cord attached to your body. It may not make sense where this cord is attached. It might be connected to your big toe, your earlobe, your elbow, or maybe you feel it sunk deep in your back or in your heart. Give yourself an opportunity to just observe this cord. Notice what material it might be made out of. Is it still or is there movement? What texture does it have? What color?

As you observe this cord, I invite you to explore what it might be connected to on the other end. Allow yourself to trust the first thought that pops into your head. It may not make sense to your mind, but we are tapping into your subconscious and your intuition here, which actually does 80 to 90% of the thinking for you. It knows more than your logical brain can process. Trust whatever comes up and comes through in this practice.

As you consider what's on the other end of this energetic cord, I invite you to see if there is one last message that needs to be either sent or received. Is there a bit of wisdom or forgiveness left? Or maybe your soul really just needs to flip it off one last time before you cut this cord and reclaim your energy and power. That's okay, too.

When you're ready and feel like it's time to cut this cord, I'd like you to imagine a hole opening up in the ground just a few feet in front of you. This hole can be as deep and as wide as you'd like it to be. Turning your attention to the spot where you can feel it is connected to you, I'd like you to sever this cord however you want to. You can grab it and pull it out, like unplugging it, or imagine it dissolving. You can judo-chop your hand through it, use scissors, a machete, or a sword like Excalibur. You can also ask your highest self, an ancestor, guardian angel, or guide to cut the cord on your behalf if you find that you need a little bit of help. Once the end of the cord is free and no longer connected to your energy, imagine grabbing it and tossing it into the hole. As you're visualizing, feel free to move your body however you'd like, pantomiming the act of cutting the cord and so forth.

Once the cord is in the ground, you can imagine gently burying it, or you can release any rage or grief you feel by stomping on it and lighting it on fire. This is your practice, and there's no right or wrong way to feel or do this. When you feel satisfied that the cord is well and truly gone, I invite you to turn your attention back to yourself and the wound where it was attached. Imagine a healing light begins to glow around this spot, and notice how it grows to encompass your whole body.

As it surrounds you in a bubble of the purest love you've ever felt, I encourage you to place your hand on your heart and take a quiet moment here to soak up this energy. Notice how the spot where the cord was has now healed, and see if you can sense how you are no longer leaking energy from there. Continue to gently scan the rest of your body from head to toe, paying attention to what has been released, what may have shifted, and what is present now that wasn't before.

Give yourself one more moment to receive any last wisdom from your practice or healing from this bubble of light. When it feels complete to you, take two slow, intentional breaths and begin to bring some movement back into your fingers and toes. Perhaps giving yourself a hug or indulging in a full-body stretch before opening up your eyes and coming back to the environment around you.

This can be a very powerful practice, and I encourage you to take a moment to either journal or voice-note the details of your experience. The minute you get up and do something else, it will start to become fuzzy in your memory, so even if journaling isn't part of your practice, I'd encourage you to capture your thoughts and feelings somehow. I also suggest that you double down on your self-care afterwards, drinking extra water, staying away from caffeine and alcohol, and going to bed early if you can swing it. You may feel extra tender or emotional during and after a cord-cutting practice – that's totally normal.

If you find yourself in a moment where you either just noticed a cord or perhaps you had a tense moment and want to clear your energy before a cord can connect, here's the 30-second version you can do on the fly. Take a moment to close your eyes (assuming it's safe to do so and you're not driving or something) and bring your arms up like you're going to hug yourself so they form an "X" in front of your chest. With a sharp snapping motion, you're going to move your hands from that "X" position down towards your hips, cutting through the energy and any cords you're feeling. Do this breaking of the "X" motion twice more, for a total of three times. Take one more moment to put your hands on your heart. I like to repeat the mantra "My energy is mine. Your energy is yours" three times to gently create a buffer zone between my energy and everyone else's. Then you're done, and you can go about your day. See? Quick and easy enough to do on the fly.

Please head to my website's Book Resources page for links to a few podcast episodes I've done around energy clearing and cord-cutting. In those episodes, I provide several powerful guided visualizations for you to use. These practices are easier to learn and practice with verbal guidance, so you can connect with my tone and pacing as I guide you through them. I highly encourage you to take a listen (and subscribe to the pod while you're there!). I also currently do this work in one-on-one sessions with clients. Details about how to work with me can all be found on the Book Resources page.

8

IF YOU "MESSED UP" WHILE TRIGGERED— WHAT NOW?

So, something happened. You got triggered, and in the moment, you reacted poorly. Perhaps you snapped at your child or fired off an angry email to the school. Maybe you agreed to an accommodation in your child's IEP that you know isn't enough, or you froze and didn't speak up about your concerns at all. Now, after you've had a moment, utilized a tool or two from the previous section, and your nervous system has calmed a bit, you realize you could have handled that better. What should you do?

Like it or not, we are all human. As such, we are going to make mistakes all the time, **especially** when something triggers your nervous system into a fight, flight, freeze, or fawn response. If, no, scratch that, **when** you mess up, there are two relationships that need some attention to "fix" or repair the situation, so let's talk about how to repair the one with yourself and the one with whoever was on the receiving end.

To start, I want to make sure that you're giving yourself grace. Remember, you are biologically programmed to respond in certain ways to threats to the safety and well-being of yourself and your loved ones. Not only that, but our primal, survival-focused brains can't tell the difference between a hateful comment online and an actual threat to your life. The subconscious level of your nervous system can't even really distinguish between a threat or disaster in front of you and watching someone else experience that threat from the intimate points of view you see daily on the news and social media. You are living with a chronically overwhelmed nervous system, which is constantly pulling blood, oxygen, and energy away from the part of your brain that thinks calmly, logically, and rationally.

If you reacted in the moment in a way that makes you less than proud later on, please do your best to acknowledge that you messed up without spiraling into beating yourself up for it. It helps me to remember that just because I make mistakes, it doesn't mean anything about who I am as a person. Good people, partners, parents, and friends make mistakes because they're human. What says more about your character is what you do about it.

This distinction is discussed by Brené Brown in her book, *Daring Greatly.* In it, she writes about the difference between shame and guilt, and how one helps drive behavioral change while the other does not. She writes, "I believe that guilt is adaptive and helpful—it's holding something we've done or failed to do up against our values and feeling psychological discomfort. I define shame as the intensely painful feeling or experience of believing that we are flawed and therefore unworthy of love and belonging—something we've experienced, done, or failed to do makes us unworthy of connection."

Following this line of thinking, do your best to stay focused on what you did (or didn't do), and what you can change so you respond next time in a way that better reflects your values. I like to reflect on the events that led up to me feeling triggered to see if there were any gaps in my self-care that might have lowered my tolerance for triggers. Was I under-rested, hangry, pressed for time, or poorly prepared? Was I overwhelmed by too much scrolling on my phone or sensory input? Yes? Then my next steps are obvious – I need to change my routine to get more sleep, detox from social media, etc.

On the other hand, was I blindsided by events outside of my control, like a medical emergency or someone coming at me in their own triggered state, which triggered me right back? Then the changes aren't necessarily in my routines, but more in having some go-to phrases in my back pocket to respond to others or a game plan for the next trip to the hospital. In these specific examples, if I'm caring for a medically complex child or an elderly parent, I might identify who to call for childcare in the middle of the night and have a hospital bag packed with self-care items for an eight-hour trip to the Emergency Room. If I'm thinking through how to respond to someone when they were triggered first, I might practice phrases like, "I see you're upset, and I will work with you on a solution when you are calm." Or, "This interaction is spinning me up, and I won't be my best self if we continue right now. Can we take a break?" You won't be able to prepare for every contingency, but now that you've identified a situation that made you stumble a little bit, it's worth thinking things through for next time.

The second relationship that needs attention after we mess up is with the other person. The good news is that experts in the field mostly agree that it's not the frequency of the mistakes that has the largest impact on a relationship, but it's the quality of the repair. Repairing a relationship usually starts with you (the person who lashed out) apologizing for what happened and for your behavior, but it also depends on the other party's willingness to accept your peace offering.

Since an apology is likely needed in most situations, what distinguishes a good apology from one that might even make the situation worse? For starters, you have to own your part in the situation. The Greater Good Science Center at UC Berkley states in their article *Making an Effective Apology,* that "apologies are most likely to be well-received if you show that you recognize who was responsible, who was harmed, and the nature of the offense." The article goes on to say that the other parts of a good apology include sometimes providing an explanation (be careful not to blame the other person), saying you're sorry, and making an effort to repair the damage done (either through changed behavior or compensation if property was damaged, etc.).

What does this look like in practice? Let's take each of the four types of trauma responses – fight, flight, freeze, or fawn – one by one to see how I would initiate repair in these different scenarios. Note: all of these examples assume at least a few hours have passed since the exchange described.

If I ended up in a heated argument (fight response) with someone at my child's school, even if I was in the "right" about the subject matter, having a tough conversation escalate to a shouting match doesn't align with how I aim to communicate with people (see Chapter 15 "Communication" under "Essential Skills – You've Got This, Mama!"). In this instance, remembering my goal is to be a leader on the IEP team, my follow-up might sound like this: *"Hi Mrs. Patel, I wanted to reach out and apologize for how things went yesterday. I clearly wasn't in the right headspace to have a productive conversation, and I should have recognized it before I said XYZ. I know you care deeply about every child in your classroom, and what I said was unfair and definitely unhelpful as we try to work together to resolve [issue at hand], and I'm sorry. That's not how I want to show up in our relationship. Can we set up another time to talk through this issue?"*

If my response was either flight or freeze, then repair looks less like an apology and more like initiating a second conversation and asking to revisit the topic. In the face of bad or unexpected news, this might look like completely dissociating from the conversation, becoming so overwhelmed that you don't absorb any of the information the other person is sharing, or abruptly ending a conversation to get away from the discomfort. In this case, my conversation/email might read: *"Hi, Mrs. Patel. I need to take a second and own up to something that happened during our conversation yesterday. When you mentioned additional concerns about Max, my mind went blank, and I'm afraid I didn't really comprehend what you said afterward. Could we set up a quick phone call to recap the rest of the discussion now that I've had a moment to process this news?"*

If, as in our initial evaluation meeting about Max, you find that you agreed to something in the moment or didn't advocate effectively for your child, this may fall under a "fawn" response. "Fawning" is a quieter trauma response and describes how people may attempt to please or de-escalate a perceived threat to maintain a calm environment and ensure physical/social/emotional safety. This often looks like agreeing to things because you don't want to be seen as a "difficult parent," spending the whole meeting focused not on the content, but in a state of hyper-vigilance to the mood in the room, or in oversharing in the effort to build a bond with the people who appear to have all the power in the room.

If you realize this is what you've been doing, I want you to remember two very important things. First, fawning is not a moral failing or personal weakness. It's an incredibly sophisticated survival strategy that many women have developed to stay safe in their families and our society. You may have been praised by others for being so easy-going, but Mama, if you're agreeing to things out of fear and shoving your thoughts, feelings, and needs into a box, that's not collaboration. Collaboration out of fear is compliance at best and coercion at worst. Either way, it's not an effective strategy for advocating for your child.

The second thing to remember is that if you now need to change your mind, trust that everything is fixable. Every IEP can be amended, and decisions can be changed or appealed. After making sure your system was grounded, your initial outreach would sound something like, *"Hi, Mrs. Patel, I'd like to revisit the discussion we had yesterday about Max's IEP. I know I initially agreed that he didn't need an alternate testing location, but after thinking it over, I think we made the wrong choice. Before you lock in the IEP, can we have another conversation about it?"*

In all of these instances, the most important thing to remember is that relationships, both the one with yourself and those with others, are "repairable." Because we all make mistakes, this rupture-repair-reconnection cycle happens frequently in both professional and personal settings. If your goal is to be the best advocate, or even just the best parent, for your child, you will need to get comfortable with recognizing your triggers and your typical responses to them, apologizing without assigning blame, taking corrective action, and not beating yourself up for the mistakes you are guaranteed to make.

9

ESTABLISH A STRONG HOME BASE

As we expand the foundation you're building outside of yourself, it's important to ensure you and your partner are on the same page. Please note that as I use the term partner to be all encompassing of your child's other parent, be it a partner, spouse, or co-parent, if you're not currently in an intimate relationship with them. You are going to need support as you walk this path, and the two of you need to present a unified front in meetings with the school. This deserves as much effort as you can put into it.

In the very beginning, my husband was doubtful that Max had any issues. Max was our first and only kid at the time, so we didn't know anything different from our family's daily normal. Growing up as the middle of three boys, Alex felt that he was just a rambunctious kid and honestly saw a lot of himself in Max. Even though I was sharing the near-daily concerns that had started coming home from daycare, Alex struggled to believe there was a problem and doubted how I was relaying the teachers' concerns.

So how did I get him to change his mind? Well, Alex is a very data-driven guy who needs to see something himself to believe it. I started by asking him to do some of the pick-ups, so he got the daily teacher's report. I made sure to at least audio-conference with him for every parent-teacher meeting and scheduled the "we gotta meet now" meetings so that he could attend in person. He has always made our family a priority, and I'm so thankful he was willing to listen. These meetings gave him the opportunity to ask a lot of questions, like, "Tell me how this behavior differs from what you would see across your classroom," or "How is this behavior impacting other students or my child's interactions with other students in the class?" These compare and contrast type questions allowed him to understand what the teachers were seeing and why it was a concern, as opposed to it just being what "high energy" boys do. Hearing directly from "experts" made a huge difference in convincing him.

If you have a doubting partner of your own, you may have to try a few things to get on the same page. First, ask them to be open to listening and learning more about what's going on with your child, and assure them you're not looking to find problems where none exist. Give them the same things you're asking from them — an open mind and a spirit of teamwork to resolve the issue at hand. Recognize (and verbalize with your partner) that you are both working toward the same goal and both want the same outcome — for the right approach and support to be given to your child so they can thrive and achieve the goal of having a happy, productive life, whatever that looks like for your child.

Also, ask why they don't agree with what you or others are seeing. You might find they have different expectations of appropriate behavior, and you need to discuss that first. Or perhaps they just haven't seen what you're talking about first-hand. My husband generally doesn't do the school/homework/chores routine with the kids. He interacts with them at the dinner table, on the soccer field, while building projects in the garage, or playing games — you know, the fun stuff — so his perspective was a bit skewed. He really only saw them when they were doing something they like to do, in a very small group setting, which hadn't given him the opportunity to observe how Max and then Henry's behaviors were disruptive both to their own ability to learn and to their peers. When he listened to our child's teachers and learned more about our son's behavior as compared to other children in the class, he agreed to have Max tested. When the results of the evaluations came back, he accepted the findings and has been fully supportive since then.

Let your partner know you value their questions. Okay, first, maybe you've got to get to a point where you actually do value their questions (hello, therapy, my old friend), but honestly, they can be very beneficial in this process. The trick here is to work on each being open to hearing both the question and the answers you find, which may or may not support your current view of the situation.

Questions must be asked in a spirit of seeking the best solution. Neither side can dig in and resist either the questions or the information revealed.

It was so easy for me to initially feel defensive, like Alex's questions about Max were really questions about **me** and my parenting. Remember, this is not about who is right. This is about figuring out what the best is for your child, which is way more important than "winning" an argument.

Just as you seek second opinions for major surgeries and medical diagnoses, asking questions makes sure you've looked at all the alternatives and considered other solutions and explanations for the behaviors or issues with which you're dealing. As long as questions are asked and received in the right way, they play a critical role in ensuring you do actually end up with the right plan for your family's situation.

So, what happens if your partner is still in denial? This is a tough one to give blanket advice for, because every relationship and situation is different. Ultimately, you've got to keep talking and negotiating until you can reach a balance point - one where even if your partner doesn't agree, they aren't standing in the way of your child getting the treatment you know they need (based on data from evaluations, etc.). I would try to get my partner to agree that I have Billy's best interest at heart and am not proposing anything that would harm him. I would also present any type of treatment as just an experiment that can be changed if it doesn't work out. *"Billy is still struggling in school, despite doing behavioral therapy once a week for the last four months. I'd like to just try medication for him, and then we can agree on a time to reevaluate if it really is the right thing. Let's experiment a bit and see if we can find the right solution, together as a family. If it doesn't make a difference, then we stop and go back to the way it was. Can you agree to that?"*

At a certain point, though, you may need to call in professional help. If you've tried all the tactics I've listed and your partner is still being difficult, then your issues may be outside the scope of my expertise and this book and I'd point you towards getting professional or legal help. But just as I've said when we've been talking about dealing with the school, **no one** knows your child as well as you do and it is **your** responsibility to move heaven and earth to make sure they get what they need to succeed, grow, and thrive as a contributing member of society. If your partner isn't on board with that, please, please consider professional couples or family therapy!

PART III

ABCS AND IEPS—EVERYTHING YOU NEED TO NAVIGATE THE SCHOOL SYSTEM

RECOGNIZING THAT EVERYONE'S JOURNEY is different, I'm going to start with a very brief overview of the process for getting support from the school. If your child was born with a specific condition, your journey may have started in the pediatrician's office. Your child may be showing signs of needing help as early as preschool, requiring you to get the school on board, possibly seeking a medical diagnosis, and coordinating services across multiple entities. Maybe your kiddo is a bit older, and she's in first grade before you realize she has dyslexia, or he's in second grade before you realize he's more than hyper, he truly has ADHD.

We will start with getting the preschool involved, and then how to start engaging the elementary school. The bulk of this section will address the Individualized Education Program (IEP) Process, and then in Part IV "Essential Skills," we dive into how to lead this team and successfully advocate for your child.

As we discuss the different meetings with the school, I can't stress enough how important it is for both you and your partner to go to every meeting. No matter how prepared you are, you will get flustered, and even with two sets of ears listening, you'll still miss key details. If your partner can't go, bring a friend or advocate. But until you've established a relationship with your IEP team, *do not* go alone!

10

HOW AND WHEN TO GET THE SCHOOL INVOLVED

If Your Child is in Preschool

Making allies with your child's preschool can be a harder prospect, depending on your individual school setting. Many private preschools or Montessori schools simply aren't set up, nor are they educated on how to handle children with special needs. If your child is attending the school district's Early Childhood Center for preschool, you may have an easier time getting support.

> *I always go into any interaction with my child's school and teachers assuming they have the best intentions at heart.*

Educators definitely don't pick their profession for the prospect of gathering fame and money! I have run into teachers I haven't liked as much, or who weren't very skilled at communicating with parents, but I've yet to find one who blatantly didn't like my child and was "out to get him." So when these experts bring something to my attention, I make sure to respond with respect and curiosity about the situation. I go into my techniques for communicating with teachers later in Chapter 15: Communication, but trust that they wouldn't say anything to you unless it was affecting the experience of either your child or the other children in the classroom.

Let's take a look at the different approaches for four different scenarios (which is an over-simplification, I know, but bear with me):

- Scenario One - your kiddo attends a private daycare/preschool/Montessori, and **they** have brought concerns to **your** attention
- Scenario Two - your kiddo attends a private daycare/preschool/Montessori, and **you have concerns** that have been identified elsewhere (or previously), and you need to get them informed and on your team
- Scenario Three - your kiddo attends a preschool run by the school district, and **they** have brought concerns to **your** attention
- Scenario Four - your kiddo attends a preschool run by the school district, and **you have concerns** that have been identified elsewhere (or previously), and you need to get them informed and on your team

Scenario One—your kiddo attends a private daycare/preschool/Montessori, and they have brought concerns to your attention.

It's easier to involve the school in this situation, since they identified the areas of concern. However, many private schools aren't staffed to handle special needs in their classrooms, nor are they necessarily knowledgeable about the resources available in your community.

When your preschool brings up issues, you'll likely have to pivot to outside resources to pursue and then follow up on evaluations, diagnoses, and treatment plans, but that doesn't automatically mean you'll need to switch to a different preschool. Ask the teachers what courses of action they've seen work successfully in their classrooms to get a sense of how far the school is willing to go to support children with similar issues. Brainstorm with the teacher to develop some potentially effective responses to behaviors so your child receives a consistent message across all settings. I'd also encourage you to speak directly with the preschool director about any concerns you may have and to keep them informed about any steps you're taking to understand what's driving any concerning behaviors and to support your child's underlying needs.

In all these scenarios, communication is key. I know many parents are hesitant to inform the school of any issues, for a variety of reasons. Perhaps they don't want their child labeled the "problem kid," or they just don't want to be a bother. Sometimes parents are still a little bit in denial, and speaking about it with someone who might confirm your fears is something they'd rather avoid as long as possible. Personally, I've never held back in sharing what we know, what we're evaluating, and what works at home, and it has never come back to haunt me. Once you've started the dialogue, you will need to work together to develop a plan for your child's future. This plan requires transparency in the communication of information as a foundation. As an added benefit, it creates a stronger team dynamic when all players are operating from the same set of information.

Scenario Two—your kiddo attends a private daycare/preschool/Montessori, and you have concerns which have been identified elsewhere (or previously), and you need to get the school informed and on your team.

If you've been noticing issues at home, likely your child has been exhibiting similar behaviors at school. So, when you approach the school, they probably won't be surprised at the topics you discuss. While I never suggest leading with a child's issues when introducing them (imagine introducing yourself, "Hi, I'm Nancy, and I have acid reflux and high blood pressure." No. Just, no.), I strongly believe that the school has to have all the important information available about your child for them to be a successful student. My mother-in-law has taught three-year-olds at a Montessori school for more than 20 years, and she's amazed by how many people drop off a child who clearly has some developmental issues on the first day of school without saying a word. It not only drastically hampers her ability to serve that child but also affects the rest of her class.

While you may be hoping that any behaviors won't be noticeable in a classroom setting or that whoever told you they had concerns about your child's development is wrong, not mentioning it early to your child's caregivers can cause harm. Children are not yet mentally mature enough to advocate for themselves. If you don't give the school and your child's teachers all the info you have, regardless of whether it's the beginning of the year or smack in the middle, then you're setting your child up to fail. Plain and simple. You must communicate with the school so they can respond to your child appropriately, with the full context at hand. Otherwise, instead of taking the time to explain things more in depth or altering sensory-heavy activities for a child with a legitimate need for extra attention, they may try to force your child to keep up with the standard classroom goals and expectations. This is a recipe for disaster and frustration, for both the teachers and your child. And guess what happens when any child is frustrated? The behavior escalates, he throws a tantrum, and guess who gets called to pick them up? You. So please, do yourself a favor and keep the school informed.

Since you've received a diagnosis, you'll need to work with the school to determine any required accommodations and modifications. You will likely have to provide a lot of information to the director and teachers who interact with your child. Many teachers at the preschool/daycare level don't have degrees in elementary education and may lack in-depth knowledge about creating inclusive environments. You will need to schedule time to bring the center up to speed on your kiddo's situation and work together on what is and isn't possible. Unfortunately, these private schools are not bound by the same laws that guarantee services and support for children with special needs in the public schools, so your results will vary widely depending on each situation.

You will also want to make sure any other staff members who regularly interact with your child are brought into the loop, too. Max had consistent issues with one aide who supported his classroom a few times a week. Once I realized she simply didn't have the same information his teacher had, I made a point to speak with her and fill her in. She had no idea about his situation and needs, and was so grateful to know so she could tailor her approach with my son from there on out.

Scenario Three—your kiddo attends a preschool run by the school district, and they have brought concerns to your attention.

When your child attends a public preschool, or one sponsored by the local school district, there may be more resources available, and the school should be better informed as to the process for accessing them. If they are bringing issues to your attention, then they likely have a plan or suggestion for how to proceed. They can recommend that your child be evaluated by the school district, and, depending on your state education laws/system, there may be different tools and resources available to you.

Here in Missouri, your child may qualify for an Individualized Education Program (IEP), which is covered in depth in Chapter 12 "The IEP Process" of this book. However, the diagnosis is an umbrella description called "Developmental Delay" and will need to be revisited again in Kindergarten. Unfortunately, with little kiddos, districts and medical providers are often hesitant to give diagnoses until they're a bit older, and it's clear that the child has a specific disorder rather than just needing to catch up with their peers. There are, of course, exceptions (autism is one that comes to mind), and if your child only needs speech therapy, then things tend to be streamlined.

The exact terminology and framework will vary by state, so I will not go into detail in this book on the different IEP categories. If you'd like more information about your state's Special Education framework, you'll have to do some online research with your State Department of Education. Many school districts will also have a Director/Assistant Superintendent of Special Education, or perhaps a Student Services Director, who is responsible for the delivery of all special services district-wide. You should feel perfectly entitled to request support from this office at any point in the process.

If your preschool has brought issues to your attention and is suggesting evaluations, consider this the best possible outcome. It means that any special needs or developmental delays are being identified and addressed early, and the school is already on board to complete at least the evaluation phase of the IEP process. (See the section on IEPs for details.) It means they are working for your child and, at this point, opening the doors to the resources your child may need. This is a good thing!

I know it can be a tough pill to swallow, to accept that your child may be outside the "norm." It's normal to see the best in your children. It's also normal to hope that any concerns or questions brought up by others (or haunting the back of your mind) are just a phase your kiddo is in and they're going to outgrow. Admitting it's not going to go away feels like a decision you can't take back, and you're stepping into a really scary new world. I. Get. It. But being in denial and not following up on things doesn't help anyone, least of all the child you are 100% responsible for. Early intervention pays such huge dividends down the road, and I promise that if you are proactive now, future-you will be thankful.

Scenario Four—your kiddo attends a preschool run by the school district, and you have concerns that have been identified elsewhere (or previously), and you need to get the school informed and on your team.

In case you skipped Scenario Two, thinking that it didn't apply to you because your child doesn't attend a private daycare/preschool, you should go back and read that section. All the things I mentioned up there apply in this situation as well - the only difference is what the school *may* be equipped to handle. Just as with private preschool, remember that the teachers and school can't provide the right education for your child with half the information. Communication is key throughout this whole process. (Don't worry, I cover **how** to communicate effectively as we go along.) I always err on the side of sharing with teachers — not to give my kids an excuse for poor behavior, but to put their behavior in the right *context*. Otherwise, teachers might not understand why your child needs to get up and move, makes noise uncontrollably, or needs extra time to finish tasks.

Any information you can give the school helps, especially as diagnoses are made. You'll need to bring the school into the communication loop so they can evaluate whether the district can or needs to provide services for your child. They may recommend that you start the Individualized Education Program process (see Chapter 12 "The IEP Process") to access necessary services, or they may suggest taking a wait-and-see approach.

Know this — you can formally request an evaluation for your child through the school at any time. This will start you on the IEP Process. If the team decides not to evaluate your child and you don't agree with their decision (aka, you're outvoted), **you can appeal this decision**. This is covered in the IEP Process section, and I can't encourage you enough to read that section with pen, paper, highlighter, and sticky flags/notes, *even* if you think you don't need to right now. You'll thank me later when you have the knowledge you need before you're in a crisis situation.

I address strategies on how to give teachers and staff new to your team an overview of your child (and how to introduce yourself without coming across as THAT PARENT) in Chapter 14 "Team Building and Leadership."

If You Have a School-Aged Child

If you read through the preschool section of this chapter, much of this will be a repeat, as the strategies and scenarios are broadly the same. There are some nuances, though, that will make this section worth your time. And if you skipped right here, you're in luck because I've got all the necessary topics covered for you.

First and foremost, I always go into any interaction with my child's school and teachers assuming they have the best intentions. I've never met an educator who is doing it for fame or money. While there have been teachers I haven't personally clicked with or who I felt were sadly incompetent, I've yet to find a teacher who was blatantly malicious or had it in for my child. When a teacher expresses a concern to me, I take it seriously and don't go into automatic denial mode. I've outlined my techniques for communicating with teachers later in Chapter 15 "Communication," but trust that they wouldn't say anything to you unless your child's issues are affecting either your child or the other children in the classroom. Let's take a look at the approach for each of the four different scenarios based on where your child goes to school and who is bringing up the concerns:

Scenario One—your kiddo attends a private school, and they have brought concerns to your attention

It's easier to get the school involved in this situation, since they identified any areas of concern and communicated them to you. However, many private schools are not staffed to support students with special needs in their classrooms, nor are they necessarily knowledgeable about the resources available in your community.

Since every school district differs in how it provides special services to private schools, I unfortunately can't offer much in the way of sweeping recommendations. What I can tell you to do is to start asking questions of both your child's private school and the local public one they would attend if enrolled in public school. You are not the first parent/family in your child's school to need access to services, so in the beginning, you may need to rely on the private school administrators and teachers for information. They brought the issue to your attention, so hopefully they're willing to work with you and guide you a bit.

I recommend being highly proactive and speaking directly with the director or principal about your situation and keeping them informed of the steps you're taking to resolve or investigate the cause(s) of the issue(s) at hand. The tricky thing here is that, since you're in a private school, they are not legally required to continue providing your child with an education, and they have the right to ask you to leave. You may very well decide that the public school or a *different* private school is the best solution for your child when all is said and done. However, I'm guessing you'd probably like to make the choice yourself and not be forced into changing things in a rush because they've told you next Friday will be your daughter's last day.

In all these scenarios, communication is key. I've never held back in sharing what we know, what we're evaluating, and what works at home, and it has never come back to bite me. It creates a strong team dynamic when all players operate from the same set of information, and it allows both parties to provide input on the plan going forward.

Scenario Two—your kiddo attends a private school, and you have concerns that have been identified elsewhere (or previously), and you need to get the school informed and on your team

If you've been noticing issues at home, it's likely your child has been exhibiting similar behaviors at school. So, when you approach the school, they probably won't be surprised. While I never advocate leading with a child's issues when introducing them (imagine introducing yourself, "Hi, I'm Jenn and I have Crohn's and anxiety." Uh…please don't.) I do strongly believe the school needs all the important information available about your child to provide a top-notch education. Guaranteed they're wondering about your child and trying to gauge when to raise the issue with you, so do everyone a favor and let them in on what's going on at home.

Even in elementary school, your child isn't emotionally ready to be her own advocate yet. If you don't provide your child's teachers with all the info you have in a timely manner, then you're setting your child up to fail. Since you're taking the time to read this, I know that's not the outcome you want for your child. You must communicate with the school so they can respond to your child within the correct context. Otherwise, instead of taking the time to explain things more in depth or altering activities for a child with a legitimate need for extra attention, they may expect your child to keep up with their peers. This is a recipe for disaster and frustration, for everyone involved – including you. And you know what happens when a child is frustrated? Undesirable behavior escalates as they try to communicate their needs, and guess who gets a call from the school? You. So please, do yourself a favor and keep the school informed.

Once you receive a diagnosis, you'll need to work with the school on any accommodations and modifications required. You will likely need to provide some level of education about your child's needs to the director and the teachers who interact with your child. In addition, depending on how your home district (the one your child would attend if they went to public school) is set up to provide services to private schools, you may need to coordinate closely with both entities.

Your active involvement could truly make or break this particular scenario. As I mentioned above, in a private school setting, they are not legally required to provide your child with an education. There is a very real possibility they could decide (without your input) that their school is not the right environment for your child. Constant and active communication, flexibility, and teamwork can go a long way toward enabling the school to provide both the education and the support your child will need to be a successful student going forward.

Scenario Three—your kiddo attends a public school, and they have brought concerns to your attention

When your child attends a public school, there are more resources readily available, and the school should be well-informed about the process of evaluating your child and accessing the resources. If they are bringing issues to your attention, then they likely have a plan or suggestion for how to proceed. They can recommend that your child be evaluated by the school district. Depending on your state's education laws/system, your child's suspected needs, and your child's age, there may be different tools and resources available to you at each step in the process.

If your school has brought matters to your attention and is suggesting evaluations, please know that this really is the best possible outcome. It may come as a shock if you weren't aware of the issues beforehand (and shame on the school if there hasn't been any communication prior to the suggestion that your child be evaluated!). However, if you can look at this as an opportunity to gather some information and not a drastic life sentence, you'll have a better frame of mind and will be more open to the results. It also means that problems are being identified and addressed, and the school is already on board to complete at least the evaluation phase of the IEP process. (For details on this process, see Chapter 12 "The IEP Process.") Since the school has come to you, you know they are voluntarily opening up the doors to the resources your child may need instead of slamming the gates closed. This is a good thing!

I know this is a totally scary new world you're entering. I. Get. It. But being in denial and not following up doesn't help anyone, least of all the child you are 100% responsible for.

I know it can be difficult to face the music, to accept that your child may be outside the "norm." It's expected to see the best in your children. It's also common to hope that any concerns or questions brought up by others (or lingering in your thoughts) are just a phase your kiddo is in and they're going to outgrow it. Admitting it's not going to go away feels like a decision you can't take back, and you're stepping into a really scary new world. Early intervention pays such huge dividends down the road and I promise that if you are proactive now, future-you will be thankful.

With Henry, in the space of one year, we went from multiple suspensions, daily two-hour tantrums, a full-time para-educator/aide, and me crying over the sink, to a successful, happy boy with less than 15 minutes per day of one-on-one aide time. Clearly, my experience is my own, but I absolutely believe it is because we were determined to identify root causes and develop successful treatment plans, and we acted as one team with both his school and his physicians. Everyone was on the same page. With hard work and a bit of trial and error, we got Henry what he needed to unlock the awesome little boy he was. Over the years, Henry has had ups and downs (please don't mention middle school to me – it's too fresh), but overall he has supports in place that help him thrive. I'm 100% sure that you will make your child's life better if you work *with* the teachers and administrators and not *against* them.

Scenario Four—your kiddo attends a public school, and you have concerns that have been identified elsewhere (or previously), and you need to get the school informed and on your team

If you skipped Scenario Two, thinking it didn't apply to you because your child doesn't attend a private school, you should go back and read that section. Everything I mentioned in Scenario Two applies in this situation as well - the only differences are what the school is equipped to handle and the fact that they can't really ask you to leave without a whole lot of justification.

Please keep in mind that your child's teachers and school can't provide her the "Free and Appropriate Public Education" (FAPE) she has a right to without all the information. I always err on the side of sharing too much with teachers - not to give my kids an excuse for poor behavior, but to put their behavior in the right *context*. Otherwise, teachers won't understand why your child needs to get up and move, makes noise uncontrollably, or needs extra time to finish tasks.

Any information you can give the school helps, especially as diagnoses are made. You'll need to bring the school into the communication loop so they can evaluate whether the district can or needs to provide services for your child. They may recommend you start the Individualized Education Program process (see Chapter 12 The IEP Process) to get access to necessary services, or they may suggest you take a wait-and-see approach.

Know this: you can formally request an evaluation for your child at any time. This will start you on the IEP Process. If the team decides not to evaluate your child and you don't agree with their decision (you're outvoted basically), ***you can appeal this decision***. While there is never a guarantee that decisions will be reversed, it does happen, just like it did for us with Max's initial denial. These safeguards and the appeal process are in place for a reason – don't be afraid or discouraged if you have to take this step. This is covered in the IEP Process section, and I can't encourage you enough to read that section with pen, paper, a highlighter, and sticky flags/notes, ***even*** if you think you don't need to right now. You'll thank me later when you have the knowledge you need before you're in a crisis situation.

11

EDUCATING THE EDUCATORS ON YOUR SITUATION

Depending on your particular situation, you'll have to do a little more or a little less of what I call "Educating the Educator." I mention it because, as a first-time parent in a daycare that offered Kindergarten, I was surprised by how much I had to teach the staff about what was happening with Max and how to best help him. Even the second time around with Henry, I had to work hard with his preschool, as everything was coming to a head. So while I can't give you hard-and-fast rules here, I'll share my two experiences and how I approached the school each time. I hope you'll be able to get a sense of how to approach your own school and its staff if you find it necessary.

Overall, I've found this effort most necessary in a preschool/daycare setting, but I can certainly imagine it might be needed in smaller private schools, and with newer teachers who don't have years of experience under their belts.

As I've mentioned, we had a grab-bag of experiences with Max. At one daycare center, they were used to working with children with special needs. They suggested we have him tested as a two-and-a-half-year-old for sensory processing issues and a speech delay (both of which he does indeed have). They were educated and supportive, and we greatly benefited from their guidance.

Then we moved the boys to a different daycare closer to home. They had experienced recent turnover, leaving them short-staffed and with some newer teachers. We had to find a new rhythm at this school, and all of us struggled until I jumped in to provide education on things I'd mistakenly assumed they already knew. Once I took on the role of educator/advocate and helped Max's teachers and the classroom aides understand him better, his preschool and kindergarten experience smoothed out, and things dramatically improved.

I highly recommend you explicitly include the classroom aides/helpers and any before- or after-school care programs in your education campaign. I remember talking to one of the floating teachers at Max's daycare when he was in Kindergarten. She was a nice woman, but Max mentioned he kept getting into trouble with her, and was convinced she didn't like him. I was surprised since his Lead teacher hadn't mentioned having any trouble with him. After working through my initial emotions and thinking about it, I had a pretty good hunch that while I had kept the director and the lead teacher informed and on the same page about Max's situation, no one had thought to fill in this woman, since she just had the kids for the after-school portion of the day. I confirmed my suspicions with the director, and then I sought out the classroom aide. Instead of hunting her down and reading her the riot act, however, I assumed she had good intentions.

I caught up with her on the playground during pick-up time one evening and said, "Hey, I know you're floating in to support the kindergarten teacher more often these days, and I get the feeling you might not have all the info you need about my son. Has anyone told you he has some special needs, specifically that he has a Sensory Processing disorder?" Her eyes got big, and she responded, "No, no one has said anything to me. What does that mean for him? Sensory processing disorder?" I gave her a quick overview and explained that's why he can't sit still, has putty in his desk, and has the exercise band around the legs of his chair. I ended by saying I hoped that having a bit more context about his struggles would help her understand his behaviors and needs in the classroom.

The entire time, I kept my tone friendly and open, and she responded in kind. I can only imagine how differently it could have gone had

I stormed up to her and said, "You're being unreasonable with Max – don't you know he has special needs? You're singling him out and bullying him, instead of supporting him. I've told the teacher all about this! I can't believe you tried to discipline him for needing to move around. What's wrong with you?" Put yourself in the shoes of this aide for a minute and imagine which one you would respond better to…the kind, open one that assumed you might just not know what you don't know, right?

A week later, she found me on the playground again and stopped to thank me for taking the time to explain things to her. She had gone to the library on her own, checked out a book on sensory processing to better support him, and said she would now start asking the front office or lead teachers questions about other kids with "behavior problems" to make sure there wasn't an underlying cause. She became a huge resource for the center, all on her own, because she recognized there was a gap in the training provided to the staff.

I was so grateful I had approached her in the manner I had – assuming she had good intentions but was perhaps just uninformed – instead of being angry and attacking her for "picking" on my child. It may be exhausting to have to explain things over and over everywhere you go, but the benefits absolutely outweigh the effort, especially when you're focused on building a solid team around your child.

Two years and a move later, as we dove into figuring out what was going on with our other son, Henry, I made sure to keep in constant contact with the preschool. I knew we were one big blow-up away from being asked to leave. However, by working hard and keeping them educated every single step of the way, they knew we were actively trying to resolve the issues he was causing in the classroom. They were much more willing to give us a longer grace period than they would have normally given a family, and more importantly, the preschool became our biggest advocates in working with the local school district to rush through an IEP so he could start Kindergarten with supports in place.

---

*The time I spent working with and educating
my children's daycare and preschool teachers
made a significant difference in the quality
of early education they both received.*

As your children get older and go into elementary school, work with the principal to ensure they are placed in a classroom with a highly experienced teacher and you'll find fewer and fewer situations where you have to teach them about how to interact with a child who has XYZ conditions. Your job as they get older is simply to facilitate the introduction of your kiddo each year, along with their unique set of needs and accommodations, to any new teachers and staff. (For more on how to introduce your child and work with new team members, see Chapter 14 "Team Building and Leadership.")

Rebe's Rules for Educating the Educator

One: Work through your emotions first. As we've already discussed in Chapter 4 "Establish Your Foundation," you are going to get triggered all the time by things the staff at your child's daycare/school does, says, or doesn't do. You must fall back on the practices taught in that chapter to work through your emotions in private. Do NOT engage the school, whether in person or via email, when you are frustrated, sad, exhausted, incandescent with fury, or what have you. Nothing good comes from that. Nothing. Work through your feelings with your partner/mom/friend, away from your child (who has to interact with this person far more than you ever will), and far away from the school setting.

If you're in the middle of a face-to-face conversation with someone from the school when you get triggered, fall back on the Micro-Meditation. You can do that mid-sentence if you need to, and then start over. You might say something like, *"I'm sorry that came out hotter than I intended it to. (pause and take a deep breath) I apologize for speaking like that. That wasn't respectful and not how I want to interact with you. Caring for Johnny has me all up in my feelings right now. I know this isn't your area of expertise and you've got a zillion other kids with their own needs, but for Johnny..."* and then go into whatever you need to say in a calmer way.

If you've fired off an email or already walked away from an interaction that you find yourself less than proud of, it's never too late to apologize. Just like when we screw up in our intimate and familial relationships, it's important to say you're sorry and own up to what you did. You can still disagree or be upset at what did or didn't happen, but nobody reacts well to being read the riot act.

It can be as simple as, *"I just wanted to reach out to apologize for my last note. I fired it off in my initial rush of feelings, and what I said wasn't respectful/collaborative/etc. No matter how mad I am or how much I disagree with what happened, I shouldn't speak to anyone like that. I'm working on it and will do better next time. I do still disagree/am still disappointed/etc. that XYZ happened. This isn't in line with the plan we have in place for Johnny. How can we prevent this situation from arising again in the future?"* and so on. See Chapter 8 "If You "Messed Up" While Triggered" for more guidance.

Two: Focus on education. When people know better, they do better. If you're struggling with a teacher who doesn't understand what's going on with your child, it's likely because they have never dealt with a similar situation before. Or if they have, and if other parents haven't stopped to fill them in on details, and what a useful response might look like, they may just not know how to help. Take the extra time to make sure that the teachers caring for your child have the information they need.

Three: Hone those communication skills! Gratitude, a spirit of seeking and sharing information, and a casual, in-person conversation will serve you well. While I usually advise parents to put everything in writing, emails don't convey tone. Having a conversation first, then following it up with an email if needed, is usually a great choice. It's very important to approach staff and teachers at the daycare or school in a way that doesn't feel like you're shaming them or frustrated that they don't know about your child's situation or how to help.

Four: Offer to share resources you found helpful when you started learning about your child's condition(s). You may want to check in with the director or principal of your child's school to see if they would prefer to share the resource(s) with their staff themselves, before you go directly to the teacher. A list of websites or books is great, but if you can, offer to loan them one of your books. Especially in a daycare setting, there likely isn't much money spent on teacher development, but you'll find teachers want to learn and support your kiddo. Help them out, and they'll be much more likely to help you and your kid out, too.

Five: Follow up. Once you've spoken with a teacher or staff member, follow up with them shortly afterward. Check in to see if they have any new questions or have new observations about your child, given the context they now have for her behavior. Repetition is important. Give the staff multiple opportunities to ask questions, and be willing to patiently review the information you've provided more than once, possibly in a different way.

12

THE IEP PROCESS

An IEP (Individualized Education Program) is a legal document for K-12 students that outlines objectives, goals, and services, as well as accommodations or modifications to the instruction or environment. This document is the result of an often lengthy process that includes the identification of a child's needs, evaluation(s) to verify special needs, and then defining what the school district will be required to provide to help the child access their legally guaranteed Free and Appropriate Public Education (FAPE). This process will include several meetings you will need to attend with a whole host of people from the school and school district before your child finally has an IEP in place — don't expect this to be a one-and-done meeting.

The primary purpose of getting an Individual Education Program (IEP) is to help your child access the general education curriculum in the least restrictive setting. In this context, "least restrictive setting" means ensuring your child spends as much time as possible with non-disabled peers in a general education setting. Depending on your child's unique situation, the least restrictive and most supportive option may actually be what is sometimes called a "self-contained" or purely special education classroom. There are a thousand ways your child's team may decide to split their time between general education and a special education setting – the point here is that the plan is tailored for *your* child and that the setting in which they will receive their education has been considered.

In this section, I'll go into a very high-level overview of the IEP process. I'll touch on each of the meetings that are generally part of the process, and then each one will get its own section later in the chapter. It's important to note that the names for these meetings or the terminology I use here might not match your state's exactly, but the general purpose of the meetings should be the same. All I can do is share what it's been called in Illinois and Missouri and give you an idea of what should happen in each meeting so you can match it up to your local process.

This section will *not* address the details of the Individuals with Disabilities Education Act (IDEA), the federal law that requires states to provide a Free and Appropriate Public Education (FAPE) to students with disabilities. There are other books you can purchase to get the nitty-gritty of your legal rights from a Federal and State level. I've referenced them in "References and Resources," but even as I write this, the landscape is changing significantly almost daily. This is an area where you will need to do your own research to determine the current process and protections in your state.

A couple of other notes in case you have skipped right to this part of the book …

First, go back and read Part II "Sanity-Savers You're Going to Need." I'm serious. That part is **foundational** for every other skill and bit of information I'm trying to share with you. Start there, then you can come back here.

As a quick overview, though, the first meeting will go a long way in setting the tone for the relationship you will develop with the main players from the school district. This relationship affects how they interact with your child daily, so it is worth taking time and care to cultivate a positive, collaborative one. In a perfect world, the meeting would be a breeze, and you would easily get access to all the supports and accommodations your child needs and more.

However, even in well-funded districts, there are limitations and other factors at play that contribute to how different team members act and react. Many of these issues are not readily apparent to us, as parents. In nearly all school districts, resources are tight, and evaluations are costly. Many administrators have to make awful decisions about who gets access to these limited services because there simply isn't enough to serve the student population.

Unfortunately, this is where this journey can quickly get really serious and tense. Think of the worst job review or feedback session you've ever had, where you were basically told you can't do anything right. You probably felt angry, attacked, shocked, frustrated, stuck, sad, and overwhelmed, right? Well, those emotions you're remembering right now are what many parents feel in these meetings and throughout this process. It can be **very** hard to hear about the things your child is struggling with and remain professional and unemotional. You may feel angry. You might be in denial about some of the things the school is telling you or worried that a label will harm your child's long-term prospects. I've worked with a lot of dads who struggle to control their temper during meetings. Me? I cry when it gets intense, and I've got 15 years of negotiation experience under my belt. I can't help it – I love my boys more than anything, and we're talking about their lives and futures in these meetings. For many, there is nothing, absolutely nothing, more emotionally heart-wrenching than hearing about how your child is struggling.

These emotions are totally normal, but they're not terribly helpful or productive. If you can prepare yourself ahead of time, know you're going to feel them, and try to hold it together as much as you can, you will be much more successful in advocating for your child. This is especially true for the angry outbursts, friend. You've simply got to keep a lid on it, unless the situation truly warrants it. Blowing up at the people you need on your side will not foster a positive, long-term relationship with them, nor will it get your child a better educational experience. Stay focused on the goal, use all the techniques and practices you learned in "Establish Your Foundation" to help you deal with a host of uncomfortable emotions, and get what you need from the school.

Start getting organized and document, document, document everything in writing (see Chapter 16 "Organization") as early as possible. It's important for you to get serious about keeping track of everything — especially if you have a sense that the school will try to avoid or skimp on providing your child with accommodations you believe they need. Get it all in writing — every last bit of it. If a discussion happens on the phone or at pick-up/drop-off, follow it up with an email to recap what was said. Casual discussions are easily forgotten, and the timestamp on an email helps to establish a timeline or emerging patterns. You can say something like, *"Mrs. K, thanks for the chat this morning. I just wanted to make sure I have the details right of what was said..."* and summarize the conversation.

And try to remember, even if you feel like you've got this, your emotions are in check, and you believe you've got a clear idea of what's going on with your child, something might catch you off guard. I want you to be prepared to walk into a meeting where you and your spouse will be vastly outnumbered. It is not uncommon for ten or more people from the school to attend these meetings. Even for people like me who routinely sit in on negotiations, this imbalance can feel very intimidating.

The amount of information you'll discuss in these meetings can be overwhelming. I suggest you bring a friend or family member to serve as your note-taker. You are entitled to bring anyone you'd like to those meetings, but be aware that some states require prior notice if an official advocate will attend. Even if you haven't hired an educational advocate, bring someone to take notes for you. Trust me on this one – you will not remember who said what by the time you get to your car.

You should walk into each meeting hoping for the best, but solidly prepared to have to fight on your child's behalf.

Decisions will be made at every meeting that affect the direction of the process, and during the meeting is not the time to figure things out! Finish reading this book, take action on the tips provided, write down all your questions, and go in smart, organized, and armed with a game plan. This way, you won't lose precious weeks like I did, figuring out what went sideways and how to fix it. You are a critical part of the IEP team and have an equal voice in the team's decisions. If you walk out of a meeting and find you disagree with a decision later, you can ask the team to reconsider, or you can appeal any decision to a higher authority. The next step in this hierarchy should be outlined in a document provided to you by the school called "Procedural Safeguards."

Step by Step: The Process

Meeting Name	Meeting purpose
Evaluation or Review of Existing Data (or Domain) Meeting	To determine whether evaluations are to be done.
Results or Eligibility Meeting	To review the results of the completed evaluations and determine Eligibility for an IEP
IEP Meeting	To set the goals and decide what accommodations, modifications, and assistive technology will be part of the child's IEP for the next calendar year.
IEP Review Meeting	Every IEP must be reviewed and updated once per calendar year, but can be revised more frequently if needed. Note these plans may span two school years (i.e. the second half of fifth grade and first part of sixth grade).

Your first step towards getting your child an IEP is to send a formal, written **Request For Evaluation** to the principal /administrator. There are plenty of good templates out there if you Google them, but for the most part, it doesn't have to be anything fancy. You will want to either mail it with delivery confirmation tracking or hand deliver it, keep a copy for yourself, and note at the top in pencil the date you dropped it off at the school and who received it. This is an important part of your documentation trail and starts the timer for the school to hold the first meeting in the process. The school is required to hold this meeting within 30 days (not school days, 30 calendar days) of the date they receive the Request for Evaluation.

Evaluation or Review of Existing Data Meeting

Evaluation or Review of Existing Data Meeting	
Meeting Purpose	To determine <u>if</u> testing is to be done
Bring with You	The Evaluation Meeting Parent Organizer, found at *www.rebegoebel.com/bookresources*, along with copies of any external reports/diagnoses and a consolidated list of issues or behaviors you've observed at home, plus any other concerns you have
Know Before Leaving	What is the decision of the team (to test or not to test). What are the exact names of the tests to be performed (if any). Who is your point of contact going forward and how to reach them. A list of Parent Resources available to you through your school district.
Your Homework	Before the next meeting, Google each of the test names you were given. Take notes so you fully understand what the test is measuring, what "average" scores look like, and what higher and lower scores mean.

At the ***Evaluation Meeting***, you and your partner (plus a friend/note-taker!) will sit down with your child's teacher, the school administration, the school psychologist, and probably some representatives from Special Education (i.e., the special education teacher(s), social worker, and/or speech therapist). Depending on your school district and child's age, your child may also be included in all or some of the IEP meetings during this process. This first meeting may have a different name in your state, but the goal will be the same - to determine whether conducting formal evaluations for special needs or learning disabilities is justified for your child. Make sure you go to my website and get the Parent Organizer to use during this particular meeting.

*Remember the main goal of this Initial Evaluation Meeting is to decide **if** testing will be done, and if so, which tests.*

As you prepare for this meeting, it's critical that you walk in organized. I discuss what to keep and several ways to get organized overall in Chapter 16 "Organization," but for this specific meeting have copies of any diagnosis your child may have received from a medical professional, a summary of communications you've had with the school/teacher to date, any reports from prior schools, and a list of your concerns from a home/parental perspective handy.

This meeting will address all potential areas of concern — grades, speech, occupational and/or physical therapy, social and emotional development, etc., and how each of these areas affects your child's performance in the classroom, both academically and socially. Each specialist will have done an initial, informal observation and will get a chance to speak. Your child's teacher will discuss what they see daily in the classroom. You will also have the opportunity to share what you've observed at home and what you view as your child's strengths and weaknesses, along with your concerns and questions.

After everyone has a chance to speak, the team will decide whether formal evaluations or testing are warranted. If the decision is yes, then you will decide at this meeting which specific tests will be done. Tests/evaluations should be identified for each area the team agrees is of concern for your kiddo.

Don't expect to know anything about the tests the team is suggesting, right now. They should all be standardized tests with very rigid guidelines for administering them, scoring them, and interpreting the scores. Use this time to ask questions about each test — What is the exact name? How will it be given to my child? What will it tell us about my child and their needs going forward? Then, when you get home, you can Google the test name to research it and start to understand what the results could look like. The outcome of these tests, when considered all together, will be what actually determines whether your child will receive an IEP.

If the decision is no, a full evaluation is not justified, then the process stops, and your child will not receive any additional services or accommodations through an IEP. This doesn't stop their access to accommodations the school provides for all children (like all children in the class can chose to work at a standing desk, or sitting on the floor, etc.), it just means your child won't have protected access to them under the law.

Know you can APPEAL any decision made by the group if you don't agree with it.

Results or Eligibility Meeting

Results or Eligibility Meeting	
Meeting Purpose	To share the results of the testing performed and determine whether the data indicates eligibility for your state has been met, therefore requiring an IEP.
Bring with You	The whole binder you've set up (see Chapter 16 "Organization") but especially the notes you took when you looked up all the tests, along with copies of any new external reports/diagnoses. Also use the Parent Organizer: Results and Eligibility template found in the Book Resources on my website.
Know Before Leaving	The results of every single test they gave your child, the team's eligibility decision (does your child qualify for special services and require an IEP or not), when the next meeting will be held and the purpose of it. You should also be given a written report that goes over all this in detail, along with the decision either at the meeting or within a day or two afterward.
Your Homework	Before the next meeting, go over all the results again. Google them again if you don't understand at a high level what they're telling you. Also, think about your goals for your child. Your next meeting will be to set out these goals and the support the school will provide to achieve them. More in Chapter 18 "Writing IEP Goals".

Assuming your IEP team agreed to do testing during the first meeting, the school has **60 calendar days** (not 60 school days) to complete the evaluations and meet with the team again. During this time, you may receive some surveys to complete, and your child will be pulled out of the classroom for evaluation. Remember, the school is working with a pretty tight timeframe, so make an effort to return anything sent home promptly. If you've received any official diagnosis from a physician since the initial meeting, I would suggest sharing it with the school *before* the meeting. No one likes surprises that could require them to change a major part of a plan with zero notice. So, in the spirit of team building, don't withhold information the school needs in order for them to have a full picture of your child.

At the ***Results Meeting*** (it may be called an ***Eligibility Meeting*** or something else in your state), the team will determine whether your child is eligible under one of the pre-defined categories for an IEP. Hopefully, the school psychologist is a kind soul and has given you an "unofficial" heads-up of what they think the data is telling the team. If you haven't heard from them a few days before the meeting, you can request this data in advance, but it's not required for the school to do so. If you're in a crap situation and you get blindsided here, I'm so sorry. You are entitled to ask for a quick break to gather your thoughts in private before you let the school start throwing all sorts of stuff at you. You need to have a clear head to do the hard work needed in this meeting.

Each specialist will walk you through the individual tests and the results, plus what those results mean. It may be as simple as, "We evaluated your child's speech both one-on-one and through observation in the classroom, and standards tell us a six-and-a-half-year-old child should be able to make this specific sound, but your child is substituting this other sound instead of saying it correctly. So we'd recommend speech services." Or, it could be messy and less clear-cut: "Your child scored in the normal range here and here, but she's off the charts over there and there. This *might* indicate that we're dealing with autism, but it's not enough for an educational diagnosis of being on the spectrum. So the best we can do is this..."

Expect **a lot** of information to be thrown at you in a very short amount of time. Ask for copies of the results of each test, if you aren't provided with them upfront, and take notes. You may want to record the audio of these meetings, so you can go back and review. The federal

IDEA law does not expressly prohibit or allow audio recordings, so you'll need to refer back to your state laws. In Missouri, you are expressly permitted to record audio of any meeting with the school district; however, many states, or even school districts, may have different statutes and policies in place. Many will make their own voice recording if you make one, so they have their own independent file.

Recording or not, make sure you understand how the data about your child compares to that of the general student population. Take your time here, and feel free to ask as many questions as you like. The results and conclusions drawn from these tests will determine whether your child receives services under an IEP or other program, like a 504 Health Impairment Plan. It's critical you understand what the team is telling you so you get the next steps right for your child.

After everyone presents their findings, the meeting leader should summarize the meeting and let you know under which category your kiddo qualifies (or doesn't) for services. Your child may have one or more qualifications — push to have them all documented now, regardless of whether any additional services will be provided. For example, if your first-grader is eligible for writing help because she has a hard time organizing her thoughts AND the scores indicate an actual learning disability in writing, the services provided might be identical in first grade, so the team might think to document only the first issue. However, as little Gabby hits third and fourth grade (not to mention junior high and high school), the services associated with a true learning disability are vastly different. If you don't document it now, while the data is fresh, you may have a heck of a time getting other schools to add in additional categories of qualification, which may significantly limit the resources available to her later in her school career.

You should be given a written report that goes over all the testing in detail, along with the team's decision, within a few days after the meeting. Read it. Make a copy and mark it up with a pen and highlighter, so you can bring it with you to the next meeting, the actual IEP meeting. Write down every single question you can think of, then go back and ask those questions after the meeting is over. In view of these results, start to think about the challenges your child faces and where you would like to see her abilities grow over the next year. Think about how the school can reasonably measure and evaluate Gabby's progress toward these goals. Yes, I know, I'm potentially asking you to do math.

But listen up, Mama, this is really important. Your involvement at this step directly affects the quality of the services your child will receive. So, buckle down and stay engaged through the end. You can do this.

Individualized Education Program (IEP) Meeting

IEP Meeting	
Meeting Purpose	To write the Individualized Education Program for your child, including goals and methods of measurement for each area of concern.
Bring with You	Any thoughts you have on goals for the areas of concern you discussed as a team during the Results Meeting, or any concerns and questions that may have come up as you and your partner have discussed things, and your completed *Parent Organizer: IEP Meeting* (found in the Book Resources on my website).
Know Before Leaving	What accommodations and supports the school is committing for your child, as well as the goals she will be working on achieving, how they will be measured, who will be doing the measuring, how often you'll get updates on progress.
Your Homework	None, besides staying in communication with the team and ensuring you receive the progress updates as agreed upon.

After your child's eligibility has been established, the school has 30 days to hold the ***IEP Meeting***. Huzzah! You're in the home stretch! Together, you'll complete the formal IEP document itself and agree on three to five goals for your child to work on over the course of the next year. You will also list all accommodations, assistive technology, and modifications to be provided or made to the general education curriculum and setting. Rarely do I agree with all the proposed goals in this first meeting, so don't feel bad if this meeting turns into two, or at least some back-and-forth afterward.

This is the meeting where you will decide if your child needs support from a para-educator, how much time they will spend in the general education environment, how many minutes per week/month they will receive specialized instruction (i.e., speech therapy, occupational therapy, social and emotional instruction), and if any adjustments are going to be made to the curriculum.

Para-educators are teaching assistants who may have varying amounts of training, but always work under the supervision of a teacher. They can provide one-on-one educational and behavioral support for children or provide secondary support for an entire classroom. Their main responsibility is to reinforce educational lessons for your child. If your kiddo has significant difficulties with attention, you may need to advocate for para services during instruction time and writing or reading blocks. Not all children require a para's support, and some may even grow out of their need for one. Max never had one, but Henry had one full-time in Kindergarten. By the start of first grade, he only had one part-time to support his behavior in certain environments (like art class and the lunchroom), and even that was phased out by the start of second grade. Other children may need two-to-one support, with both a full-time para-educator and a full-time nurse to support their complex medical and educational needs.

Accommodations and supports are adjustments made to the general education learning environment to support your individual child in participating as fully as they can in that setting. In general, you can think of accommodations as falling into a few categories: altering what's expected of a child to produce, changing how that child will do their work, changing the level of support a child receives, adding assistive technology or tools to support them, and changing how a student is taught.

For altering what a child is expected to produce, the IEP team might suggest that your child's assignments be shortened or the expectations reduced. If your child struggles with getting their thoughts down onto paper, an alternate way of demonstrating mastery of a concept/topic might be proposed, like the teacher engaging your child in a discussion about the assigned reading to get verbal answers to questions instead of writing a three-paragraph essay. If your child needs extra support, they may be placed in a co-taught classroom, where there is an additional teacher, usually trained in special education, or they may get individualized instructions from their teacher. Assistive technology and other supportive tools encompass a wide variety of items, including a braille typewriter, communication boards for non-verbal children, visual timers to keep kiddos focused, and sensory tools, like weighted blankets and fidgets. In some instances, it is in the child's best interest to receive specialized education in particular subjects, like adding lessons for a child in social and behavioral skills, or even switching out the standard reading curriculum for one that is tailored for a child with dyslexia.

If your child has complex needs, you and the team may also discuss whether the general education setting is the best place to meet their needs. This is a multi-faceted decision that should never be taken lightly, nor is there a right or wrong choice here. Most experts agree that, in general, having a child integrated with their peers is beneficial to a child with special needs...until it's not. Only you know if your child will be too overstimulated, if their medical or behavioral needs simply can't be met in a classroom with 20 other children, or whatever reason you have for knowing your child won't thrive in a general education classroom. This meeting is the time to discuss how much time your child will spend in general education, as well as the special education setting, which includes all the time they get pulled out for speech, occupational therapy, or other specialized instruction the team agrees your child needs.

Accommodations will vary widely from child to child, as they should be tailored to *your* child's needs. For example, with Max his accommodations included the freedom to move around the classroom to work in different locations, the ability to use a predictive spelling/writing software, permission to chew gum, the opportunity to take tests in a distraction-free environment, the use of headphones to listen to music, extended time on assignments and tests, and once our school put in a sensory room, he was allowed to request a break during the day to visit and use the items in the room to support his nervous system. However, Henry has very little overlap with his older brother's accommodations. Henry needs support in organizing and tracking his assignments. He gets a copy of teacher-provided notes for class lectures, and he also needs to use earplugs in noisy classrooms and communal areas.

As the team discusses goals, accommodations, and supports, make sure they truly reflect your kiddo's strengths and challenges. Don't be afraid to ask not only for what you think might support your child, but also ask a million questions about why the team is recommending what they are. With my two boys, I remember the team wanting to reduce the complexity of the reading assignments because they both struggled to get their thoughts down on paper. I refused to let them simplify these assignments that way because those two stinkers were reading three to four levels above their peers, and they could tell you every nuance and detail of what they had read. They didn't need simpler reading assignments; they needed a way to demonstrate what they knew verbally. As a team, we landed on taking videos of me asking them the questions from the assignment instead of them having to write it all down, and all of a sudden, their English scores went way up because we changed **how** they could do the assignment.

During this meeting, you will also establish the goals your child will work on for the next year. Chapter 18 is dedicated to "Writing IEP Goals", so I won't go into the details too much here. There are, however, a few things that you need to know going into this IEP meeting and about goals in general.

First, keep your eye on the big picture — your vision for your child's future. All the goals outlined in the IEP should support your child in learning the skills they need to be successful as an adult, however that may look for them. While your first priority should be to have clear, precisely written goals that align with your vision and your child's current needs, rest assured that you can request a mid-year revision if needed.

Second, know that *you* have a say in the goals that are written for your child. I've seen schools present prewritten goals to parents and then resist making any changes to them. This is not okay. Writing the goals for your child should be done collaboratively with the whole team, and *you* are part of that IEP team. You have every right to ask questions and suggest not only modifications to the proposed goals, but also completely new goals. Remember, while the others on the team may have degrees in education, they aren't necessarily expert goal writers. This is a level playing field.

Third, don't rush this step. Each time we've created a new IEP or needed to overhaul an existing one, this meeting has turned into two. IEP goals are critical, so we take a lot of time to ensure the goals are written correctly and have sometimes needed extra time to research what was proposed by the school.

Lastly, remember that the goals you write this year will likely not be the same goals your child is working on next year. They are not set in stone and should be updated whenever you or the IEP team feels it's necessary – even in the middle of the year. If you realize mid-year that your child needs more or less support than you thought, or that the data you're getting back isn't actually telling the team what you need to know, call an IEP meeting and update or amend the goals section. Even though writing the goals is a critical step, mistakes can always be fixed. That's it! You've done it! Well…almost…

IEP Annual Reviews

IEP Update or Review Meeting	
Meeting Purpose	To review the IEP for your child and/or make updates as necessary.
Bring With You	Any thoughts you have on both the current goals and suggestions for new age-appropriate goals to add. If your child's medical situation has changed, hopefully you've already communicated it, but have any documentation ready in case you're asked for it. Use the Parent Organizer: IEP Annual Review worksheet found in the Book Resources on my website.
Know Before Leaving	What the new or updated goals are, how they will be measured, who will be doing the measuring, and how often you'll get updates.
Your Homework	None, besides maintaining regular communication with the team and reviewing scheduled updates on goals.

While I'm sure you were hoping you'd be done once and for all after the IEP meeting, you'll have to review that newly established document at least once per year, or whenever any member of the IEP team (including you) requests to meet. The whole IEP team will get back together again for an annual IEP Review Meeting, where you'll discuss your child's progress toward their goals, anything new that has come up, along with what might be age-appropriate now, and then you'll adjust the goals for the next year accordingly.

The IEPs for my kiddos are due in November and January, respectively; however, I received calls from their schools last week about updating both their IEPs sooner rather than later. Preparing for two IEP meetings to be held on the same day is just twice the fun, right? (<--insert sarcasm font. Ahem.) While it might not be anyone's idea of fun, because I have a process in place and communicate with the school frequently, I wasn't surprised, and I am not panicked about getting ready for either of these meetings.

One other note, every few years, the school district will have to reevaluate your child to determine if they are still eligible for an IEP. In my area, it's every three years and is typically rolled into that year's annual review. The school will review all the current information on your child, and they may readminister some or all of the evaluation tests used in the initial evaluation. They will then present their findings to you, along with any suggested changes to your child's IEP. This extra piece and discussion may make this meeting longer than a regular annual review meeting.

The preparation for an annual review meeting will be largely determined by a few key factors: How do you feel about the services your child received over the course of the last year? Has anything major changed for your child (like a new diagnosis)? How are things different for your child this year vs. last year (for example, are there any new problems arising from different social and educational expectations that weren't present last year)? Do you feel like the data being collected is sufficient and accurately measures progress (or lack of) towards the IEP goals?

The first thing I look at is how I feel my child is doing and what might have changed since the last time the IEP team met. I review how things are going at home and write down my kiddo's strengths and the things they have worked hard to improve. Seriously, write these positive things down at the top of your paper in bold. Holding the positives and progress made at the forefront of your mind will help you approach this meeting in a better frame of mind.

If anything new has come up, I write it down along with some rough, brainstorm-type notes on how it may influence existing goals or require the team to consider a new one. If there's a new diagnosis, I make sure I have a copy of the letter from the physician or psychologist and get it to the school/IEP team **prior** to the meeting, if I haven't already given it to them. And to be honest, I'd probably have a backup copy of it with me no matter what. Just as you don't want to be surprised in a room full of people, let the IEP team know about any critical updates before you walk in. Not only does this foster the "one team" feeling, but it's simply more efficient. You'll be able to spend the precious minutes of the meeting talking about the goals, not giving a bunch of updates.

Next, I pull out the current IEP document and remind myself of exactly what the existing goals are. Because I make routine communication with the school a priority, I typically have a pretty good idea of where my child is in achieving the milestones in his goals. But, as I've said before and will say a million more times, knowledge is power - so I want to know that document from cover to cover when I'm sitting at the table with the rest of the team. I make notes about where I think we are for each goal, whether we should keep it as written or not, and what the milestones should look like going forward. Then I brainstorm language for any new goals I'd like to see incorporated.

The actual meeting agenda will vary, but in general, it will start with updates from you and your child's current teacher. They'll share what is and isn't working and what they think should be provided or changed for the year to come. The specialists will review the IEP goals and the data they've been tracking to determine which goals have been met and which your child is still working toward. They will recommend which ones should be removed, changed, or added, and you'll get a chance to provide input as well. The IEP team will review the supports, accommodations, and assistive technology currently provided and suggest appropriate changes. Once everyone is in agreement, the school will finalize the language and send a copy home for you to review and approve. After that, you're set for another year. Hooray!

PART IV

ESSENTIAL SKILLS— YOU'VE GOT THIS, MAMA!

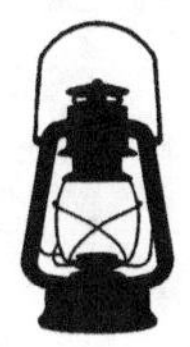

13

ASSEMBLING YOUR TEAM

THINK OF THE SUPPORT STRUCTURE you need to build around your child as a three-legged stool, with your child seated on top, firmly and evenly supported by each leg. The first leg of the stool is you and the rest of your child's family. The second leg is the medical community, including your child's pediatrician and, of course, any specialists they see. The third leg is the school. Children are most successful when they have solid support from their school (both general education and special education), open-minded and proactive medical care, and parents who are active and engaged in every step of the process. Let's talk a bit about all the players who were critical to my own journey, so you can start to think about who you'd like to draft onto your team.

You and Your Family

In order for you to be strong as a parent, you need to have a solid inner circle of supporters, period. Regardless of whether you've got a child with special needs or not, parenting is a tough and often lonely road, requiring what sometimes seems like an endless supply of patience under the most trying of circumstances. But the minute you suspect your child has special needs, *you* need to get yourself some extra support and get loved ones on board — quickly.

Your inner circle will likely include family members, but don't discount others in your community. When I started this journey years ago,

I lived several states away from family who could help out. These days, we have seemingly unlimited ways to connect despite distance; however, with a special needs child, you will need someone local to pitch in from time to time. You may need someone to watch your child's sibling(s) while you take him to therapy or another doctor's appointment. You may need someone who can babysit all your kids, including the one(s) with special needs, on occasion. Above all, Mama, you'll need someone who understands the whole situation, someone to cheer you on and bring you brownies on the bad days.

I've always been outspoken about our journey and challenges, knowing intuitively I needed these strong connections so I could give everything I have to my children. This transparency and candor have brought me unexpected relationships and opened doors I never even knew existed. I'm not suggesting you dump your struggles on everyone within earshot, but for those who have earned your trust and especially if they have similar experiences, share your story with them. The more open you are, the more you can get connected to resources you never even knew existed for both yourself and your child.

So where might you meet people in your community? One sure-fire way to meet people who will immediately understand your situation is to join a local support group for families of children with the same condition(s) your kiddo(s) have. Many of these meet in libraries, through your local Children's Hospital, or online, and will immediately connect you to parents who have already traveled in your shoes and can guide you as your family starts down this path. They will have suggestions of medical professionals to see (or avoid) and can speak to the kind of supports their child received through the school system.

You may also find support through getting involved with local or even national non-profit agencies. A quick online search for "support for families with special needs children" returned over 100 results. Here in St. Louis, there are a plethora of foundations and other groups whose main purpose is to support families like mine and yours. Not only can you find support and build a community for yourself, but your child will be able to connect with others just like them and may even find wonderful activities and opportunities to participate in as well.

Last, but certainly not least, check out online forums or groups. I've found great, helpful communities in several Facebook groups as well as websites designed specifically for families of children with special needs. These are wonderful places for asking those hard questions that you'd hesitate to ask someone in person, like, "Am I a jerk for thinking XYZ?" or "How do you handle it when your family is unsupportive?" The beauty of finding support online is its 24/7 availability. Regardless of what time it is, someone else is also online, and you can get immediate (albeit crowdsourced and unprofessional) support and guidance.

With all of these options, you will have to take the first step and reach out, even to your own family, to let them know you need help. Resources, supportive communities, and new friends are abundant if you look for them. In the beginning, you may feel completely isolated, but if you just look around a bit, between the people who already know and love you and the ones you meet along the way, you'll find you're really not alone.

Medical Community

Your medical team will likely start with your child's pediatrician. They, in theory, know your child the best and can recommend or provide official referrals to specialists in your area. While this book isn't focused on how to manage the needs of medically complex children, the skills you'll find in this section are all still applicable. The unfortunate truth is that just as you need to assume a leadership role on your child's educational team, you have just become the keeper of the medical file, too. You will need to be proactive and organized to ensure that medical decisions are being made with all the current, necessary information. Use what you learn here to create a team mentality among your child's medical providers and to fold them into the larger community you're building to support your kiddo.

Rebe's Rules for Working with Medical Professionals

One: Make any and every appointment you think you might need right away. Specialists in my area have over a six-month wait list, so make all appointments immediately after you get a referral, even if you may end up canceling it later.

Two: Once you make the appointment for six months out, **ask to be placed on the waiting list for cancellations**. If you can be flexible, ask to be called if there's a no-show appointment, and you can reasonably get there within 15 minutes.

Three: Go into every doctor's appointment with a list of concerns and questions written out, just like you would approach a business meeting. Additionally, make sure you have updated lists of medications/procedures done and copies of any letters of diagnosis from other doctors.

If your child is medically complex and has a large team of specialists, you may even find it helpful to create a medical binder. Yes, even in today's world of online medical records, I highly recommend keeping physical copies of lab results, diagnosis determinations, referrals, etc. Like it or not, medical professionals are moving quickly and can make major mistakes or simply will not believe what you're telling them. Documentation that **you** have easy access to during appointments can dramatically improve your child's outcome in many circumstances.

Four: Consider setting up a parent-doctor only meeting. This is incredibly helpful if the situation is complex enough or your children require too much hands-on attention for you to be able to focus and understand what the physician is telling you. I did this when Max was about two — I simply couldn't pay attention to the doctor **and** keep him from pulling all the stuff off the walls or out of the cabinets. So I asked the doctor if we could connect for five minutes on the phone later, which worked out much better. We also did this several times as my son got older, so we could discuss concerns without him overhearing us list our issues and concerns about behavior, etc.

Five: You are the one who has to ensure that information gets from one professional to another. Overshare information. You can't rely on overworked office managers remembering to fax test results over to a different office, nor can you rely on the other office to receive and get that data into your child's medical record. This may require sending update letters or messages via the patient portal between visits. But there is great benefit in allowing doctors to consult with each other and having a bigger pool of knowledge to pull from. You never know when a seemingly unrelated piece of information will be the key to a physician knowing what's going on.

Five-b: Repeat/overshare information during visits. Ensure your physician has reviewed the documentation that's been sent over. This is where a medical binder can help you out. If you have a copy of the results/diagnosis/etc. then you can hand it to them so they can skim it right then and there instead of digging through the patient portal.

Six: Ask questions. Tons of them. Use my favorite one, "Help me understand…" in every appointment. I also like, "Have you considered…" as well as, "Can you walk me through your thought process on choosing that medication/treatment/diagnosis/etc.?" Medical professionals focus on their area of expertise and have limited knowledge in other areas. Remember, they "practice" medicine — they don't know everything. You should never be afraid to ask for a second opinion or to question recommended therapies. If a physician tries to make you feel bad for asking questions, then you need to report them to the practice manager and find a new one if at all possible. If not, bring backup to subsequent appointments, record the discussions, and use the tools you're learning here to try to improve a tough situation.

Within the disability community, there are different theories around therapy and whether it is actually helpful or harmful for children to participate in. This is a topic you will have to decide for yourself, but I do want to make sure you're thinking about what will set your child up for long-term success. Will this child with cerebral palsy ever be able to walk? No? Then why force them to keep trying when you could move on to teaching them how to navigate the world with assistive technology? Will this autistic child benefit from speech therapy? Yes? Then go for it! But don't hesitate to ask these questions before you start.

Seven: Do your own research, but be very careful when Googling things! At one point, Henry's psychologist was concerned he might have a specific neurological disease. We looked it up to know enough to agree he should be screened, but I was very conscious not to Google the condition in depth, staying away from blogs, support groups, etc., until we had a diagnosis in hand. I'm so thankful I held off, because the whole thing was a false alarm.

Eight: You know your child best and are the only person 100% focused on **them**. You have to be the #1 advocate for your child, not only in the school system, but also within the medical community. Trust your gut and fight for your child with everything you have.

Nine: If you feel like your questions/suggestions aren't being taken seriously, find another doctor. If you have limited options, do your research, find peer-reviewed studies that support your view, and request the doctor review the evidence and your child's situation again with an open mind.

The School

Now, let me briefly talk about how to approach the school. Most of the book is dedicated to the nuances of working through the school to get the resources your child needs, so I'm going to share one brief analogy here. Then I'll let you dive into the rest of the skills you'll need to effectively build a long-term collaboration with your school district.

Years ago, I attended a Parent Leadership Institute for parents just like us. Much of the value in the Institute is found in listening to others share their experiences and viewpoints and learning from them. One mama told the story of being a Labor and Delivery nurse. She said couples would come into the hospital with concrete plans for how they wanted their delivery experience to go — play this playlist, everyone should whisper, the diffuser should be pumping out lavender-scented mist, and absolutely no drugs. She shared how many women would be dead-set on their personal vision and fought against the medical advice they were being given as their labor progressed because it deviated from their plan.

She, as one of the knowledgeable players in the room, said it was hard to feel like she was on the same team with these women who were discounting her years of experience for a plan they had dreamed up outside their current reality. Women with "hard and fast" birthing plans inevitably ended up being disappointed when things didn't happen the "right" way, even if it was for the safety of their own child.

She went on to say that by contrast, expectant mothers who approached labor and delivery with informed preferences, as well as a spirit of collaboration and flexibility, had much more pleasant experiences and were significantly easier to work with as a nurse.

You can apply this second approach to your child's school. Approach the teachers and administration with preferences you can discuss, not concrete demands you refuse to deviate from. A flexible attitude honors both their years of experience and the fact that you know your child best. It fosters an even playing field, leading to an environment where a team mindset develops, and you can work collaboratively to form and develop a plan for your child.

14

TEAM BUILDING AND LEADERSHIP

ONE OF THE ABSOLUTE KEYS to this whole life you've been thrust into is learning how to lead and collaborate with the team you have. You'll get to pick some members of your team, like private doctors and therapists, but within the school system, you'll largely have to deal with whoever is assigned to your child. And remember, some of these team members will change at least yearly. So you need to get comfortable quickly with building a team and working well with people — even the grumpy ones. In this chapter, I'll go through some textbook team-building philosophy and then add in my own two cents on **how** I've applied it in my life.

One of the things the Air Force quickly teaches young officers is the Phases of Building a Team. The phases are Forming, Storming, Norming, and Performing. I'm sure you've seen them firsthand on any team you've been a part of, be it at work, in a club, a volunteer organization, or the Parent Teacher Organization at your child's school.

In **Forming**, the team meets for the first few times and starts working together. You'll outline roles for each team member and the goals the group is trying to achieve together. Here, people are trying to learn about each other and are sizing each other up to get a sense of where they fit in the dynamic.

Storming is the second phase of team-building. Just as its name indicates, this is a rocky, turbulent time for the group. Disagreements will arise as to who is and should (or shouldn't) be doing what for the team. People will become unhappy with their assigned role or perceived place in the power hierarchy and jockey for a different position, either openly or in an underhanded way. There may be flare-ups of temper and heated arguments, depending on the nature of the team and the goals you're trying to achieve.

Once the dust settles, the group will go through **Norming**, where a new normal will be established, and people will accept and relax into the roles and tasks they have to play on the team. There may still be a few bumps in the road, but in general, these will be met differently and more calmly than during Storming. This is the start of the group really pulling together and working as one.

Then comes the magic of **Performing**. You've found the sweet spot, and everyone is working well together. The team is in sync and producing what it needs to deliver on its goals. This is the ideal state for any team.

During any one of these phases, you may find a team member needs to be replaced if that person simply can't work well or fundamentally doesn't agree with the methods used or direction the team is headed. As one of the key members of your child's team, you have every right to ask for someone else to be put on your team. However, I have two big caveats here: First, you have the right to ask that someone be removed and replaced, but you may not get what you ask for. You do not have the right to make that decision yourself (within the school setting). You'll have to have a solid case as to why you need a replacement team member, and then you'll need to work with district officials to make that happen.

Which leads me to my second caveat: Don't make hasty decisions here. This should not be your first response to issues that come up with team members. That is to say, not everyone who disagrees with the team at any point in the process should be removed. In fact, disagreements and respectful discussion about alternatives are healthy and desired! This is how you find out about new ideas and can take advantage of creative solutions, so don't shut down all dissent. But if there is an obstructive or destructive person on the team who you truly feel doesn't have your child's best interests at heart, it's okay to ask that they be replaced.

If you've read this book straight through, some of this will already be familiar to you, as a team-building approach colors all my interactions with the school. But if you've flipped right to this section, I'll lay it all out here for you.

My training in the Air Force taught me a lot about building a team in the crappiest of situations, where every day was about preparing for upcoming wartime deployments. As you can imagine, the atmosphere right after 9/11 was tense, and the military has no shortage of big personalities all trying to be an alpha-dog. Building a team and keeping morale up was challenging, to say the least, but over my years of service and subsequent management roles, I honed my approach to interacting with people one-on-one and to pulling them together to achieve a bigger objective.

Before we get to my personal rules of team-building, let me give you a little pep talk in case you're feeling like an imposter or that you don't know enough to help your child. You **<u>must</u>** believe you have an equal place on the team as the teachers and school administrators. In the beginning, I know it's hard to feel like you deserve a voice and opinion in how the IEP is developed because you're acutely aware of how much you don't know about the process. But you are a mandatory part of the team for a reason — regardless of how much time your child's teacher spends with them, they still don't know them as well as you do. And their goal is to balance the needs of all the children in their class.

You have one job, Mama, and it's this: Move heaven and earth to get your baby what she needs, so she can thrive and grow and become a contributing part of society.

You are the **only one** at that table who is 100% laser focused on your child and you have to get smart and get comfortable speaking up, fast. If all else fails, Fake it until you make it, Sister.

Rebe's Rules for Team-Building

My number one rule: No matter the situation, approach people as if they want to do their job to the best of their ability and appreciate them for doing it well. Treat them respectfully, including learning and using their names. The key to all of this is to approach people with a spirit of gratitude that they are there to help you with whatever you need.

This rule actually works regardless of the situation you're in. That's why it's my first rule! Start practicing this approach the very next time you need something from someone in any customer service role, or from someone who is the gatekeeper to what you need. Try it the next time you call the cable company, mail a package at the post office, or visit Starbucks. Smile, thank them for keeping their cool with the huge line they've been dealing with, and **then** ask them for what you want/need. This rule makes normal, non-stressful interactions more pleasant, but more importantly, it diffuses tense situations. You can be as pissed off as you've ever been, but likely the person you're going to interact with to try to fix it is NOT the one who made you mad in the first place. So be nice to them; otherwise, you're just dumping on someone who probably doesn't deserve it. And even if they are the source of your issues, if they are also the one who has the power to fix it, you **will not**, I repeat, **_will not_**, make anything better by attacking them or going into the conversation convinced it's going to be a battle.

In the school setting, remind yourself that no one goes into education for the money, fame, or to mess up as many kids as possible. The men and women who work in our schools do it because, at one point, they fell in love with teaching children. I know I would lose my mind in a classroom with 20 five-year-olds all day, so I approach every conversation with my children's teachers from that spirit of gratitude — I'm so thankful they're doing what they're doing! That doesn't mean miscommunications won't happen, or that you won't find a mismatch between your child (or you) and their teacher. Just as you have dated people who are perfectly nice but not your cup of tea, you'll have teachers you like less than others. But you can still be thankful they do what they do for you and your kids. If you start every interaction with gratitude, I promise you're well on your way to building an amazing team.

Two: Lead with curiosity and gather the facts of a situation before you make a snap judgment. Never is this rule more important than in a school setting when you hear something that just doesn't make sense fly out of your child's mouth at the end of the day. Case in point: Max came home with a poor grade on a science test. I asked him about what had happened, and he said, "Well, I go to Mrs. W's room (the special ed teacher) during science every day! I miss all of science every day! How am I supposed to know this stuff if I'm not in the room when it's taught?!" and he stomped off in a huff. Oookayyyy.

Now, clearly, I needed to check in with the teacher to see what was going on, and I had two choices when I sat down to write her an email: I could be pissed and accusatory (*"How is my child supposed to do well on a test when he's never in science for any of the instruction? It's unfair and puts him in a horrible position! What am I supposed to do? Teach him science for you this year??"*) Or I could get curious about what was going on in the classroom.

I bet you know which one I picked, right? I started asking questions, and my actual email read like this...

"Hey, Mrs. B. Sorry to email you so late in the evening, but Max just shared something with me, and I think I need some more information about what's going on. I was just looking at the science test you sent home, and Max said he did poorly because he misses science class every day to go down to the special ed classroom. Can you fill me in on what his day looks like? Does he miss science every day? And if he does, can we chat about alternatives? I know your days are bonkers [*using Rule #1 here, too - Gratitude/acknowledgement*], so please feel free to either email me back at your convenience or I'll be up there after school tomorrow in the library if you want to chat face to face. Thanks so much for helping me clear this up! Rebe"

In the end, it turned out that Max did miss the last five minutes of science every day, which, in his mind, was significant. But his poor grade was really due to a lack of studying, not to missing instruction time. Regardless, we all worked together and agreed they could shift his time in the special ed class by five minutes. This was all worked out over four or five very polite emails with zero fuss. I know for certain that asking questions instead of making accusations will always deliver better results.

Three: If you're going to be a leader and build a team around your cause, you must be prepared and organized, which includes looking the part. This is covered in more detail in Chapter 16 for "Organization" and Chapter 19 for "Negotiation." Here I'll simply say that in my own career, I've always had more confidence in the leaders who looked polished, were prepared for meetings, and were organized. If you want to be a leader on your child's IEP team (the answer to this is YES, right?), then you will need to spend some time the night before you head into the school getting yourself put together, both physically and mentally.

This is all about the role you need to play in the meeting and the image you want to project. It's simply human nature that by being organized and dressing in something that boosts your confidence, you will be perceived as on the same playing field as others, giving you an equal seat at the table. If you show up looking disheveled, you'll lose this advantage.

Four: As a leader, it is your responsibility to be as objective as possible. Try to keep your emotions under control. Many things may be triggering as you travel this path for years to come. Yes, this is an emotionally stormy situation you're in, I totally get it. Yes, I've cried in IEP meetings. I've also been absolutely furious with the key players after things went sideways for us, but I never shouted or said anything that was less than professional to their faces — in private, you do what you need to do! I. Get. It. You can be firm and express displeasure without yelling or being nasty.

We've all had bosses who have reacted emotionally, or even worse, unpredictably, to tough situations or hearing bad news. You didn't like working for that boss, did you? It probably made you anxious every time you had to talk to him, because you never knew how he was going to respond to what you had to tell him. Don't be that person. Be the one people look forward to working with, because a school is a small community, and you want next year's teachers to **want** to have your child in their class because they know you, as the parent, are easy to work with and are enjoyable to be around.

This is where you put the tools and practices we went over in Part II "Sanity-Savers" to use. In case you skipped it, stop right now and go back to read it. I cover what you can do before, during, and after tense situations to support your nervous system. This is **foundational** to your ability to advocate effectively for your child.

Five: Take a time-out if you need to pull yourself together. Before making a big decision, have you ever said, "Well, let me sleep on it, and I'll let you know in the morning?" If you have, you took a time-out to give yourself the space you needed to make a calm, rational decision. The same principle applies here. If you aren't sure that the IEP team is heading in the right direction, ask for a break. Are you getting upset in the meeting and worried you might say something you'll regret? Step into the hall for five minutes to calm yourself down and gather your thoughts. Not sure that the IEP goal makes sense? Stop working on that one for a while and come back to it, even if you have to have another meeting or phone call just to finalize it after you've played with the language/metrics/run test scenarios/etc. I've said it before, but it bears being repeated — your emotions **will** run high at some point. Recognize it before it gets out of hand and know you'll actually gain respect from the rest of the team for asking for a break if you need it, as opposed to losing their respect if you lash out at them.

Six: Be willing to compromise. While you may have to insist on some things, in general, I find that being open and flexible whenever possible fosters goodwill with the school. I try to be supportive of what the teacher needs for their classroom to function, but firm when advocating for the accommodations or assistance my child needs within that same classroom.

If I find a teacher is resisting a suggestion or request, I fall back on Rule #2: Lead with Curiosity. I start asking lots of questions like, *"Help me understand what part of this request makes you hesitate or would be difficult for you to implement in your classroom?"* or *"I see that you're not a huge fan of this request. I'm trying to ensure that Max has access to assistive technology so he can keep pace with his peers. If X isn't an option, have you seen or used something else that would achieve the same goal?"* Get creative and see if you can find a middle ground that both of you are comfortable with.

Seven: Finally, for the love of all that is holy, remember this last rule. Be polite and respectful. No one wants to work with a difficult, rude person. Nor do jerks really get better outcomes for their children. Because if you're the one screaming at a teacher over whatever it is that's sent you over the edge **_again_**, that negative association with YOU will carry over in how they react to your child. No matter how awesome they are, they're human, and how you act will color how they respond to your request and to your child's needs. Even if you have been absolutely backed into a corner (see Chapter 21, "How to Act When It's Bad" for more advice), you must stay respectful and professional if you want to effectively advocate for your child and build a top-notch team that will work for them willingly, not just out of obligation.

A New School Year Means a New Team

Sadly, no matter how awesome this year's group of teachers and staff is, next year will bring changes to at least the homeroom teacher your child has, and at times a total overhaul of the team if your child is switching schools. This can be a silver lining if you have had a less-than-helpful person on your team, so it's not always a bad thing!

Between our move to a new state and all the transitions that have come as my boys have grown into the young men they are, I have a bit of experience in getting a new team up to speed quickly. The beauty of the system I use is that it's flexible enough to work in a variety of settings, including summer camps or after-school programs. As they've gotten old enough to advocate for themselves, I haven't had to follow this formula as tightly, so remember you can adjust what I share to work for you and your kiddo.

Step One: Send intro email. If your school is like mine, you likely won't know until the last minute who your kids will have for teachers, but the minute I get a name, I swing into action. I drop them an email introducing myself and my child, and requesting the opportunity to bring my kiddo by before the school's official meet and greet time. But there's an art to the content of this email that's worth taking a page or two here to go through.

First, I express excitement for the year to come and thank them in advance for all the time and energy they're about to pour into the kids over the next nine months. I always lead with gratitude, regardless of the subject I'm emailing them about. Always.

---

*Pro tip: thanking them before the hard work begins
makes them more likely to work hard for you.*

Many (ahem, *many*) years ago, when I was transitioning from military life to civilian life, I used one of the nation's top recruiters to find my first corporate job. It was highly competitive to work with them; they accepted only the top 20% of applicants, and they worked with me for six months before the interview conference I was scheduled to attend. This conference was a herculean effort to coordinate up to 16 interviews per candidate over two days, preceded by two full days of info sessions for each candidate on each company they'd meet. I know, it boggles the mind, right? During the prep work leading up to the conference, I sent the team a huge box of brownies and cookies from this amazing bakery in LA to thank them for the effort, *regardless of my own personal outcome from the conference*. I wanted them to know that even if I didn't get a job from the whole crazy ordeal, I recognized and appreciated the effort they were putting in.

When I got to the conference, the company's owner was standing at the ballroom entrance, greeting each of us individually. As I introduced myself, this absolute grizzled hard-ass of a man gripped my hand in both of his and exclaimed, "My dear, are you the one who sent us the box of treats last week?" I admitted I was, and he told me that in 30 years of working with the top military officers from all four branches of service, he had received many thank-you gifts *after* someone had accepted a job offer, but never *before*. "That was one hell of a classy move, Rebecca. Well done." And Roger continued to check in personally with me throughout the conference.

Out of the sea of 100+ candidates, plus the thousands he had coached over his career, I had stood out because I expressed my thanks upfront, before they put in a huge amount of effort on my behalf. I'm convinced that people will work harder for you if you adopt this approach, not only because they feel appreciated, but also because you've set the expectation high in such a way that they **want** to work hard for you and your family. (And yes, I got multiple job offers at the end of that process, and nearly twenty years later, I'm still in contact with some of the recruiters I worked with to get them, though sadly Roger passed away.)

Okay, back to writing that email. After thanking them for doing what they do, I introduce myself and my son using a worksheet I created (which you can download from my website). The "New School Year Transition" guide was designed to give the new teacher or staff member the key information needed for day-to-day interactions at their fingertips. IEPs are generally these huge, dense documents that use very formal and structured (ie, limited) language. This is your chance to give the people who are going to be key players in your child's life the CliffsNotes® version of Sally's triggers, what it looks like before they blow, and past successful strategies for dealing with each situation. It's a page or two they can tuck into their desk for their own quick reference as they get to know Sally, and it's a fantastic resource they can share with the PE teacher, the recess monitor, and any substitute teachers they may have over the year. (FYI, you may have to give them permission to share this document with other staff in the building. By this point, you know my position on this — You should absolutely give it! Make sure all the people who interact with your child have the key pieces of information they need to help your child be successful in all the school environments!)

Two tips for filling out this worksheet: One, do at least a rough draft at the end of the school year when all the year's strategies are fresh in your mind; and two, I also highly suggest you get last year's teacher to give you some classroom input for this document (yet another reason to do it right at the end of the year, instead of just before a new one starts). Then, finalize the document with any changes that happened over the summer, just before you send it to the new team. This gives the new staff not only a parent's view of their children, but the practical advice of the educator who spent all of last year working with your child.

I also take a line or two in this email to let them know what to expect from me. When things were harder for my boys, I would tell them they're likely going to hear a lot from me until we establish the new working routine for the year, and then, as long as things are going well, I'll fade into the background. I let them know my goal is to first and foremost support my child, but also to support them as the teacher. I promise to always get their side of any story I hear at home and ask that they do the same for anything they hear at school. I let them know that I truly view the IEP team as a **team** of which I am a willing and active participant.

I also ask how the teacher prefers to communicate. Most teachers these days prefer email because we are all constantly connected; however, I always stress that regardless of when I send a note, I'm not expecting an immediate response. If something is that urgent, I'll pick up the phone and call. Especially for notes sent late at night or over the weekend, I'll start with, "I don't expect you to respond until sometime Monday/tomorrow, but I wanted to send you this note while I was thinking about it. Here's what's going on…" Some teachers are open to texting, but that has typically only been offered after we've established a solid relationship and I've explicitly gotten the ok, or if they are using a classroom texting app. Texting is much less formal and is harder to keep organized as part of any documentation you're keeping, so for anything important, it's better to stick to email.

Next, I state our requests for an early one-on-one meeting and any special accommodations I know we'll need right off the bat (standing desk, being allowed to have gum, etc.). Then I wrap up with a positive closing, reaffirming our excitement for the year and the opportunities we will have to work together to make sure my child thrives in their classroom.

Step Two: The early "meet and greet" for you and your child with their new homeroom teacher/core staff. My guys both had a bit of social anxiety in new situations and with big transitions when they were younger. In elementary school (or preschool), meeting the teacher early, while they're setting up their classroom for the year, was so helpful. Some years we've been able to go in a few days before the school's official "sneak peek," and other years it's happened 30 minutes before everyone else shows up for the meet-the-teacher event. Regardless of when it happens, I've found it a helpful step in the team-building experience – giving my kiddo a bit of time to get comfortable with a new person and environment, without peers around, and me a chance to chat with the new teacher. This has also been successful for starting summer school and summer camps.

Besides the obvious benefit of giving your child a chance to get a feel for their new environment and teacher in a less overwhelming setting than the "sneak peek" your school may host, this is an opportunity for you to follow up in person and demonstrate you meant what you wrote in the email you sent the teacher.

Please take special care with this first interaction with your child's teacher. I recently spoke with a woman whose son has autism. We talked about how the whole system can be impacted, positively or negatively, by a parent's relationship with the school administrators and teachers. She described how she used to go to meet-the-teacher nights at her son's school, and when introducing herself to the teacher, she'd say, "I'm the mother of the brightest student in your class," then wait to see who the teacher guessed was her child. This mother felt she was being playful; however, I guarantee her son's teachers felt like she was trying to trick them right from the very first moment. Think about it. There is no good way to respond if you're that teacher. While this mom thought she was being clever, she absolutely did more harm than good. This is not the time for cleverness. If you're straightforward and clear in every interaction with your child's school, you'll be surprised at how quickly a positive relationship can develop.

Step Three: Follow up on anything discussed during your first meeting. Depending on how the meeting goes and what you discuss with the teacher face-to-face, you'll want to send a quick follow-up email thanking them for their time and then confirming any details afterwards. Remember, documentation is always the name of the game and covers everyone's behinds. So let's assume you asked for X, Y, and Z in your first email and then during your discussion with the teacher, you changed one element. The two of you agree on X and Z, but he suggests that Q might be a better option than Y this year. You should summarize all those points in a quick email to the teacher. It serves as a reminder for the teacher who is trying to learn a lot of students at once, a communication check between the two of you, and documentation in case you need it later in the year.

Step Four: Call IEP team meetings as needed (different from full IEP meetings). Anyone on the IEP team (including you) can call team meetings as needed. These are meetings of key IEP team members, but they are NOT official IEP meetings. Official meetings have defined purposes set by the State Board of Education and are listed under the IEP Process section. These, however, are just update meetings, and you get to set the frequency of them with the other team members. During one critical time period with Henry, I met daily with the general education teacher at pick-up time, got daily behavior sheets, and also met monthly with the special education teacher and the behavioral specialist. As time went on and we had a solid plan in place and working for Henry, we were able to dial back the frequency of all those touch-points.

The goal with any of these steps isn't to overwhelm the new teachers you'll be working with, but to start the important process of team building and to establish yourself as an active, supportive participant in the education of your child. These building blocks are critical to the foundation necessary for effective collaboration and negotiations down the road.

Remember, you are also building your reputation within the school district. Teachers talk amongst themselves, just as much as any other group of humans do, and it's a pretty small community no matter where you live. Be nice. Be supportive. Be grateful and appreciative. Feed the troops. Get the help you need along the way. It's as simple as that, friends.

One last thought: If there is any way possible, volunteer at the school. Becoming a presence in the school and giving back go a long way towards building yourself a positive reputation. This said, I recognize that not everyone has the ability or capacity to volunteer. There have been times when I was able to spend hours a week on volunteer projects. There have been seasons where caring for my kids and aging parents left me with no gas in my tank for anything else, and I had to step back from non-essential commitments. I also want to recognize that I have benefited from the privilege of having a salaried job, a husband with a salaried job, or being self-employed, so finding the time to be involved is easier for me than for others. It just is, and I want to make sure I acknowledge it.

If you have no flexibility during the day to be in the school, but have the capacity and desire to volunteer, see if you can pass out programs for the evening winter concert, or go in before work one day a month to make copies for the kindergarten teachers. If time is scarce, but you can spend some money, send some snacks over for the teachers' lounge with a card. I promise it will get eaten and appreciated! Find a way to use your talents for the benefit of the whole school/class, not just for your child, and you'll see how quickly it works in your favor.

15

COMMUNICATION

Your journey likely began in one of two ways. Either your child has special needs that were apparent at birth or shortly thereafter, or after a few years and a few different teachers commenting on the same "issues" in class, you began to piece together that there might be something bigger going on for little Kevin. Looking back, I can vividly remember conversations with each and every set of daycare teachers Max had about his energy level (which is HIGH, my friends. HIGH.) and how he gave them all a good "run for their money." At the time, we wrote it off as just him being a little boy, but as the conversations continued, we started to pay closer attention. We started asking questions like, "Help me understand how his behavior differs from his peers," and "How does this affect your ability to teach and the ability of not only our son to learn, but the other children as well?" Once we hit first grade and the days were more structured, we really began to notice an increase in issues and communication from the teacher.

If you start to see a pattern or an increase in the conversations with your child's teacher, either verbally or over email, start to keep track. Save all the emails in one folder or jot down notes about what the teacher brought up (see Chapter 16 "Organization," for ideas on how to track this info). When you have a few collected, review them to see if any patterns jump out.

Maybe you're having issues at home and wondering if the teacher sees the same behaviors in the classroom. Open and honest communication will benefit all parties involved — you, the teacher, and ultimately your child. When both the teacher and parents are on the same page, then the child receives consistent structure and guidance, which can, in and of itself, improve behavior. Regardless, sharing concerns and strategies for dealing with undesired behaviors is a good thing.

It's worth noting that your communication with the teacher may differ in tone, formality, and cadence from that with school administrators. They play different roles, and so your communication style may flex accordingly. The general education teacher can be your child's greatest ally, both in their daily interactions in the classroom and during the IEP process; however, recognize that they are just one voice on the IEP team and likely don't have final say over any decisions that are being made about your child.

Rebe's Rules of Supportive Communication

One: My golden rule of communication boils down to what I would tell any of my airmen or employees: **Keep me in the loop on important topics and never surprise me with bad news or something I needed to know in front of my peers or my boss.** Tell me as soon as you know so we can be proactive with whatever response is necessary. I figure that if this is what I ask of the people who work with me, then it's only right that I treat my boys' teachers with the same respect. Provide people with the information they need to do their jobs so that your child gets the best education possible.

Two: Be transparent with the people who spend more time with your child while they're awake than you do. There really isn't any benefit to keeping vital information about your child from the school. All you do is slow down the arrival of the accommodations and support you're trying to get for your child if you don't give them a clear picture of what your child is dealing with and therefore needs. I have never hidden who they are and what they need from any school, and I believe this open dialogue has allowed me to gain access to resources more rapidly than others who have dripped out information, leaving the school to guess at what is going on with their child.

I kept our teams in the loop on things large and small. This helps the teacher connect with your child and may even avoid an unnecessary meltdown. When Henry was little, I shared, "Henry hates stickers with a passion, but loves everything orange. Can you put an orange star or smile on his papers instead of a sticker?" I would also share when he had a rough night or was already two meltdowns into his day at 9 AM. And recently I had to reach out to the school to let them know we were really worried about Max's mental health and suspected it was impacting his coursework.

Three: Make sure you are communicating clearly and often with the school. The "right" amount of communication exists on a continuum, meaning the "right" amount will change over time. You'll find you need to tailor the frequency of interactions (both in-person and electronic) to the current situation's needs. When things are changing rapidly, your communication should ramp up as well. For example, when we were first starting Henry on some new medications, we were tweaking his dosage every four days or so. EVERY time we changed it, I sent a quick email to the school nurse, his homeroom teacher, and his special ed teacher so everyone was in the loop and could keep an eye on him for unwanted side effects. I would also send his teacher a note if I discovered too late in the morning that he hadn't taken his medicine, just so she has some context for any changes in his behavior. I always over-communicate at the beginning of a new school year, for example, and as we settle into the year, my check-ins with my kiddo's teacher taper off. I usually see an uptick again mid-year as I check in on the progress he's making and to see if anything needs to be tweaked for the second semester. Then I cross my fingers and hope we have smooth sailing until summer break!

Four: If you have any concerns, always err on the side of formally documenting them. Write them down in a concise email to the teacher with a clear purpose. Are you asking for their advice/help with the situation? Do you have suggestions you'd like them to consider? Do you need their input before you visit your child's pediatrician or before you start the formal evaluation process? Make the purpose of your communication clear, give the important details/backstory, and ask for their assistance in resolving the situation.

Five: Start and end the conversation with acknowledgement and gratitude. Let them know you see how hard they work in the classroom or how much you admire their grace under pressure, or just how much your child enjoys having them as a teacher. Find something **genuine** you can compliment them on here. This isn't about being slimy and trying to butter them up; they'll see you coming a mile away. But, if you can be authentic in your appreciation for the job they're doing, they will be much more likely to keep an open mind and hear you out when you address the information you need to share with them. I always thank customer service people for helping me out, and even when they say, "Oh, I'm just doing my job," my response is always, "That may be, but it doesn't mean I'm not thankful for the awesome job you're doing for me." This approach darn near guarantees good service every time I call.

Six: Keep an open mind when communicating with your child's teacher. Try to understand the limitations the teacher may be working under, as well as their responsibility to all the other children in their classroom. They are very likely bringing up issues because they're concerned about your child and are doing their best to keep a classroom full of squirrels focused on the same thing at the same time. If they can't do exactly what you're asking them to, ask what else might work in their classroom.

Seven: All my communications follow a pattern ingrained during my years in the Air Force and working with senior executives. **I will tell you what I'm going to tell you, tell you the details, and then tell you what I told you.** It sounds redundant, and it is, to some extent, but bear with me for a minute here. We are all drowning in emails, right? Well, so are your child's teachers. This formula helps busy people quickly understand what you need from them. They can skim the details and then respond accordingly. When you bury the request or point of the email in the middle of several paragraphs of rambling details, you'll find it takes longer to get the responses you need, **or** that you've confused your audience and now require another email exchange to clarify, and so forth.

For example, you might write, "Hi, Mrs. Smith! I'd like to quickly get your input on the summer programs I'm looking at for Sarah. (*Bottom line - I need your input.*) I know you've got a good handle on things in the classroom and would love to steal a bit of your expertise. (*Genuine compliment and gratitude.*) We're looking at these three options, but I have XYZ concerns. (*Details go here.*) What are you seeing in the classroom these days that I should bring up when I call the directors of these camps next week? (*Asking again for the input you need in summary.*) Please feel free to email me your thoughts, or I'm happy to stop by right after school gets out on Tuesday for five minutes or so."

Eight: Make your email subject lines crystal clear, like "Update on John's medications" or "Input needed regarding summer programs for Sarah." This way, when a teacher quickly scans her emails, it's obvious which ones she needs to prioritize. Then structure your note following my trusty formula. Remember, you want the main point you're making up front, then the details/backstory, then a quick summary to wrap it up.

Nine: Any time the teacher is telling me about an issue or concern, I always seek clarity, facts, and perspective before I respond, regardless of the situation. Much of this is because I recognize that the teacher has a very different environment and set of interactions than I do with my child. I ask for clarity and additional facts by using phrases like "Help me understand…" and "Can you give me some additional information about…" before launching into an interrogation. For each instance, I try to get the answers to: What was going on just before the incident occurred? Was the class transitioning to another activity or location? Was anything else out of the normal routine? Did the teacher see the event unfold or just hear about it from another child? Your approach here **must** be one of seeking knowledge, not seeking ammunition to turn it back around on the teacher. Tone and intent will convey a clear message — if the teacher feels attacked, you won't get the clear picture you're seeking, and this interaction won't help build the support team you want.

I find that I learn a lot and build strong relationships by asking for people's perspectives. Remember, these professionals see your child for more waking hours of the week than you do and in a totally different environment. Behaviors often differ in response to the unique demands placed on them by a school setting. Asking questions like, "Help me understand how Jack's reaction to this request is different from the rest of your class" or "You're telling me that he's falling behind the standards for this grade at this point in the year…how far behind is he compared to his peers?" or "Can you tell me a little bit about how this behavior affects your ability to teach and the ability of those around him to learn?" All these questions (and answers) help you see your child in a different light and give you a measuring stick. Especially with your oldest, and assuming you don't have a huge family with tons of kids, you may only have that one child to use as your point of reference. I had no idea little boys could sit still until I had Henry. I only knew Max and what his standard behavior/energy levels/etc. were. Asking about what the teacher sees in general across the age group will help you compare and contrast what **you** see and gain a greater understanding of your child and what needs to be done to support them both in school and at home.

Ten: Follow up like it's your job. Keep track of the details in your notes, set reminders in your phone, whatever you need to do to keep track of things that need to be confirmed. We lost track of an accommodation we had verbally requested (the ability to wear a single earbud and listen to music during class) during Max's annual IEP Review. The team agreed that he had been doing it informally for years, and it wasn't disruptive, nor was it negatively impacting his ability to learn, so it was supposed to be added to the documentation. However, we forgot about it, they forgot about it, and it was never written into his IEP. Fast forward to the summer of 2025, and Missouri passed a law banning the use of any personal electronic communication devices for the entire school day. We reached out to his case manager to determine the procedure for accessing this accommodation through his IEP, only to find that it was never documented. And now, the school understandably cannot grant a new accommodation that violates a state law. Had I taken better notes during the IEP meeting and double-checked them before skimming and approving the draft IEP, his usage of an earbud would have been grandfathered in and retained. I got sloppy in my 12th year doing this, and unfortunately, it is negatively impacting my son and his ability to concentrate. Learn from my mistake and make sure you follow up and follow through on any requests you make of the school.

<h1 style="text-align:center">16</h1>

ORGANIZATION

IF YOU'RE JUST GETTING STARTED on your special needs journey, you will probably feel totally overwhelmed by all the information you suddenly need to keep straight. Deep breath, Mama. We've all been there. However, I can promise you with absolute certainty that getting a system up and running as soon as possible will achieve three key benefits for you. First, it will save you time later when you inevitably need to refer back to a piece of information. Instead of scrambling or wasting time hunting through your email, stacks of papers, and files on your computer, you'll know right where to look. And second, your nervous system can settle when you know where everything is. Being organized is a proactive step you can take to remove a stressor from the process. Finally, you can trust that the school has its documentation in order. Having your own ducks in a row shows them that you are taking an active role on the team and should be treated as an equal and serious participant.

In this section, I'm going to break it down into **what** you need to keep track of and a couple of proven methods for **doing** so. This may seem overwhelming at first, but getting started early means you can try a couple of methods and find what works for you before you have a mountain of papers or digital files to convert from one system to another. When in doubt, start with something simple and a method or tool you're already familiar with. This is not the time to learn a completely new software system, although I understand the allure of a tool that promises to solve all your problems. Please also trust me when I say that just keeping everything in your email inbox is not a good solution either.

What to Keep

At a minimum, you'll want to keep information on both the education/school process and any outside or medical data about your child in the same place. Remember, we're trying to get all the different groups of people supporting you and your child to function as one team with one purpose, even if they're never actually in the same room together. In order to do that, you have to be organized so you can share all the information with others. The items I keep can be broken down into four main groups: Communications, Results/Data, Medical, and Reference Materials.

Communications with the School – Most likely, there has been some back and forth between you and the school about the concerns you're either seeing at home or the teacher sees in the classroom. You need to pull these together into one place. The name of this game, especially with the school, is to **document, document, document** everything. If they are already in email format, go back through these emails (sent and received) and consolidate them (either digitally or in hard copy; see below for a couple of options).

If you have just had verbal communications with your child's teacher, summarize everything you've talked about over the past few weeks and send it all to the teacher in an email. You might say something like, *"Hi, Mrs. Smith, I've noticed we've had several conversations about Billy, and I just want to make sure I have the details straight and in one place. I'm hearing from you that Billy is struggling with XYZ, and it is impacting his education/your classroom in these ways...Have I summarized the situation as you see it correctly?"* and ask for a response via email. This then becomes the start of your document trail.

Start doing this after every conversation with the teacher. Type up a quick email recap of everything you two discussed and send it to them for confirmation. Even if they never reply, you can use it to build your case (if necessary) because it does two things for you. First, this email trail establishes the frequency of issues your child is having in the classroom. Second, if they never correct what you've written to them, you can assume (or at least argue) they agree with your summary of the discussion had. This is powerful ammunition, should you ever need it.

If you send or receive any formal letters from the school, keep dated copies for your records. These could be letters of discipline or suspension, or letters requesting that the school provide resources or an evaluation for your child. Email is how most of us do business these days, but in education, a formal letter carries weight and meaning that emails do not. Formal letters are often included in a child's permanent file, which will follow them to their next school. Make sure you keep a copy of **anything** you mail or physically drop off at the school, along with noting the date and who received it. Given the state of the mail system these days, you may want to consider sending any formal requests with tracking or even certified/signature required so you have iron-clad proof of receipt. This isn't required by the process per se, but in a contentious situation, it may be the right thing to do.

I also recommend starting a Contact Log and putting it at the front of whatever system you use. Catalog every discussion you've had up to this point, and then be diligent in logging all future conversations as they happen, as well as adding the content (printed email or copy of letter) to this section of your files.

Results and Data – You may not have much to add to this section right away. As you get further into this process, you will want to gather or start to keep track of copies of any diagnostic tests from the school and medical providers, along with report cards, progress reports, or any other routine general education tests that might indicate issues are present or developing (i.e. weekly reading tests that show Jane isn't keeping up with the progress her peers are making or standardized testing results showing where your child is in comparison for their age/grade level). You will also want to keep notes from all IEP meetings with the school, as well as all the forms and the packet of papers they provide you at any meeting you attend. Lastly, this is the place to put any other information you believe helps you make your case to the school or should be tracked long term.

Medical Information – This section might be your biggest or your smallest, depending on how medically complex your child's needs are. I have a few lists or charts I've created to keep track of information that is hard to keep straight in your head, but that you will need to refer to frequently and share with both family and the school. The first is a timeline, where I have noted important dates and the who, what, and where details. For example, on Henry's timeline, I list all the dates of the different surgeries he's had, what was done (ear tubes, adenoids out, etc.), by which doctor, and in what facility. The second chart lists each medical provider, their specialty, and their contact information. This way, not only do I have a handy reference for who is who, but should I be unavailable, my family members will have that information immediately accessible. The last chart I keep is for current medications. I track the name, dosage, pharmacy it gets filled at (local or mail-order), and the doctor who prescribed it. Writing it down means I can free up precious brain space, and again, it means someone else can pick it right up and support my child if I'm not able to.

Reference Materials – The last category of information you want to gather and keep long-term is Reference Materials. This includes any research and information you've gathered on your child's specific needs (so I have info on the local Tourette's support group, along with links to ADHD articles in Henry's info), as well as general information about Special Education. You might include research on the Federal and State laws governing education, any Parent Handbooks put out by the school or your district, copies of the school district policies and procedures governing Special Education, as well as a guide to your district's IEP process, if one is provided.

While the documents I've listed here are by no means an exhaustive list, you should now have a solid understanding of the types of information you should keep organized. If you've been gathering it as you go, I'm sure you've amassed quite a stack. Now, let's get it all into a format that is easy to maintain and gives you access to the information you need quickly.

How to Keep It All Organized

There are a million ways you can organize all the papers you're going to be flooded with in the coming weeks. I tend to err on the side of keeping everything, which makes it even more critical to have a system to track it all. At a high level, you'll have to make a choice between keeping things digitally or in an old-fashioned notebook. Personally, I use a hybrid approach that leans more heavily on the digital side. The fact of the matter is that documents are transmitted digitally, and there will be a **large** volume of information you will need to keep track of that will eventually span over a decade of your child's life. Unless you just love the idea of a row of file cabinets in your home, you'll likely need a hybrid solution as well.

Digital Solutions

There are many, many ways to get yourself organized digitally, including Google Drive, Notion, Trello, OneNote from Microsoft, the Notes app on your phone, Evernote, and the list goes on. Personally, I use Evernote because I've been a paid user of the platform for well over a decade, and I'm familiar with it, so it's a no-brainer for me. Remember, don't let the tool you choose add stress to your life! This isn't about getting things perfect. You just need to be able to find stuff when you need it.

Regardless of which digital tool you choose, let's take a step back and think about the system you're going to set up. At a minimum, you'll need to keep track of email correspondence and attachments, physical letters sent to or from the school, grade cards, testing reports, perhaps letters from medical professionals, links for support organizations, and random screenshots from your camera roll.

As you consider which digital solution you want to start with, pay attention to how easy it is to get these different items all consolidated into one place. Can you forward emails directly into the tool? Can you save multiple types of files, such as audio recordings of meetings alongside the notes you took? Can you save photos and screenshots? PDFs and other attachments?

Once data is in the tool, how easy is it to access? Can you get your information across various platforms so it's available on your Android phone, iPad, and your computer that runs on the Windows operating system? Can you log in on a web browser? Can you share things easily with your partner or other caregivers? How easy is it to get info back out of the tool if you need to print or otherwise share with medical providers, etc.?

Once it's in the tool, can you organize the data, documents, and notes into groups or folders to add some structure? How searchable are the data and files you save? Will it scan and turn handwriting into searchable text?

Regardless of which software or app you choose, practically speaking, I just can't see how you can avoid needing to keep track of digital information. And these days, you can almost completely get away from paper in your long-term storage of information by using either one or a combination of a few digital solutions. For me, Evernote ticks all these boxes, so I keep paying for the premium membership, but I completely understand that it's an expensive subscription, especially if this is the only thing you would use it for. I love the powerful search capability, and having all the current information available at my fingertips on my smartphone means I don't have to lug in a giant binder and shuffle through hundreds of papers to find the one thing I'm looking for.

Old-School with a 3-Ring Binder

You may not be comfortable keeping important papers organized digitally, and that's okay! Luckily, the same skills that got you through school will come in handy again as you set up a binder to house all the papers coming your way. To get started, buy the biggest heavy-duty binder you can find, plus a 3-hole punch, and pocket section dividers. You may also want to have some small sticky notes, a highlighter, and pencils handy. It will only look too big until you start to gather your information – trust me, it will fill up quickly.

Just like in Evernote, there are many different ways you could set up your binder. The Wrightslaw book, *From Emotions to Advocacy*, by Pamela and Peter Wright, includes a whole section on how to set up your child's comprehensive file. They recommend you organize all documents by year, placing the date in the corner of each piece of paper, lightly in pencil. They also recommend you put the oldest documents on top, with new information filed toward the back of the binder. That doesn't work for me personally, but given how respected this book is in the special needs community, I'm sure it works for many people to file things this way.

I started out with *From Emotions to Advocacy* as my go-to reference, so in the beginning, I set up a physical binder "by the book," so to speak. However, I quickly found their system didn't work *for me*. For one, I think in categories, and having correspondence mixed in with test results made me twitchy. I also found it inconvenient to flip through every document to reach the back of the binder with the most recent files. Plus, I found the notebook to be heavy, hard to search through, and difficult to maintain. These are all reasons why I switched to a hybrid digital and paper solution, using Evernote as my main repository.

If you want to use a straight chronological filing system, I would recommend you reverse the order suggested by the Wrights and place the oldest documents on the bottom of the binder, on the right-hand side, and build "up" from there with newer files.

If you want to use a physical notebook but prefer separate sections, I'd recommend starting with a Correspondence section. Create a Contact Log to track phone calls, email correspondence, and face-to-face conversations you have about your child with a few details. Then add the actual paper copies of these interactions behind the log, again placing the most recent ones on the top of this section. I suggest you then add four more sections for Medical Info, Evaluations done by the school, Research, and Formal IEP Paperwork with your meeting notes. Again, within each section, file everything chronologically with the newest documents on top.

One last tip for any official documents you keep physically: Make copies of all reports and mark "Original" in pencil at the top of the original. Then mark the others as "Copy" and scribble all over them with your notes and questions. Always keep the original clean in case you need to make additional copies to provide it to another entity.

Hybrid Digital and Paper

While I use Evernote 95% of the time, I do keep some things handy on paper for specific periods. I like to have test results printed, with extra copies for the team, when walking into a meeting where I know they'll be used or shared. I take most meeting notes on paper as I find flipping open a laptop or tablet, or typing away on your phone, can still be seen as disrespectful in some academic circles. However, that attitude is slowly changing, especially since COVID normalized having IEP meetings via digital platforms like Zoom or Google Meet. Depending on your state, you may or may not be able to record audio during meetings with the school. Right after the meeting ends, I open Evernote on my phone, snap a picture of my notes page, and file it in the right kiddo's Notebook. Additionally, I scan all the documents provided during the meeting using either a desktop scanner or an app on my phone, which converts photos to PDFs. Doing this right away means I have peace of mind – no more worrying about a lost random post-it or piece of paper the school psychologist handed me with a kids' meditation app she recommended scribbled on it.

This hybrid solution also allows flexibility depending on where I am in the process. I found over the course of setting up four different IEPs, having some critical pieces of information available on paper was more useful early in the process (during Eligibility and Evaluation meetings) and less important once an IEP was established and working well.

Getting organized is an absolutely critical step in the process, but I don't want you to get overwhelmed. I know it feels important to get this right from the beginning, but the truth is, your system not only will, but **should** flex with your needs. You can easily play around with a couple of different methods, especially early in the process. Eventually, you will settle into a system that is right for your brain and your specific situation. The keys here are to gather everything up, pick a method, get everything you already have in it filed/uploaded, and make it part of your weekly or monthly routine to update whatever system you create. No matter how you decide to file things, keeping it updated is your first priority.

17

HOW TO PREPARE
FOR MEETINGS

I PREPARE FOR ANY IEP MEETING the same way I did when negotiating multi-million-dollar deals. First, I get all my facts straight and gathered. Next, I think about what the other side may want or might bring up, and what my possible responses would be. Then I think about what my goal is for the meeting and how that might be affected by what the other side's goal is or what I've already considered they might address in the meeting. I make sure to write down any questions so I don't forget them during the meeting. And finally, I get my head and heart in the right place (see Part II "Sanity Savers").

Depending on the purpose of the meeting you're preparing for, the information you need to have gathered and organized will vary. I go into detail on what you'll need to have gathered for each meeting in Chapter 12 "The IEP Process," but in general, you'll want to have a summary of communications you've had with the school between the last meeting and this one, in addition to any documents or diagnoses you may have received from non-school entities (physicians, private evaluations, etc.).

Once I've gathered my information, then I think through what I know and what I suspect will come up from the other side, in this case, the school district. The amount of time this step takes may vary from a minute or two to an hour to game-plan. I've included my general thought process below, but taking a couple of minutes to read through

Chapter 19 "Negotiation" will also be very beneficial as you prepare for meetings with the school.

Overall, you want to think through and even write down your answers to the following questions:

- What are the key topics, goals, or decisions that need to be made in this upcoming meeting? This includes topics that are key to both sides.
- How do *I* feel about each of these items? What would my best-case scenario outcome be for each of them?
- What do I believe the school wants for each of these outcomes?
- What is the worst-case outcome I'm willing to accept? This is known as your walk-away point, where if you don't get at least this minimum level of whatever, you would shut down the meeting and "walk away." In a school setting, this would look like recognizing that the assembled people aren't going to come to an agreement, either ending the meeting or moving on to other topics, and then appealing to the next higher level in the food chain. I go over this more in the Negotiation chapter.
- Looking at this list of topics, goals, and decisions, what are my top three, and which ones are less important? Rank them from most to least important *to you,* and then repeat the ranking from the school's perspective.
- Looking at this list, where are there holes in the information I have at hand that I could gather before the meeting? Does or will that information change my best-case or worst-case scenarios or my importance ranking of the item?

As you go through this list of questions, you may want to create a chart to keep it all straight. You can find a sample one, including one that is blank and one that has been filled out with example answers, in the reference section at the end of this book.

Finally, you'll want to get your head and heart in the right place before the meeting. Every meeting is a negotiation, and you've got to have a rock-solid mindset when you walk into the school because it has the potential to be an emotional rollercoaster. Hearing about new problems/concerns, setbacks, or a lack of progress on some goals has the potential to push parents into a negative spiral of denial, blame, shame, and anger. NONE of these are productive emotions and will not help you advocate for your child at this meeting. Yes, they are valid feelings. Yes, we have all felt them. Yes, it sucks, and we're all sad for at least a moment or two that our child has to work harder to do things most everyone else takes for granted.

But I know one thing for a fact — if you're taking the time to read this, **you** are an awesome parent who is doing your best. Your child's lack of progress toward meeting goals does not mean you haven't been proactive enough as a parent or are doing anything wrong. It is not a personal reflection on you; it just is what it is. If your child isn't meeting goals, you need to ask the IEP team some hard questions about the goal (is it written correctly to measure progress? Is it appropriate for your child's situation? etc.), or you need to get more creative in the support being provided to your child to achieve it. But try really hard not to let these discussions bring you down.

For me, getting my head and heart in the right place can take a couple of forms, depending on what I need. I covered most of my go-to practices in Part II "Sanity-Savers You're Going to Need," so I'm not going to go over them all again. However, here are a few things that have worked especially well for me over the years; remember, you can take or leave what you like. In general, my recipe looks like this:

Preparation + Sleep + Healthy Movement + Quiet Time + Fuel = A Mama Ready to Kick Ass

---

Preparation: We've covered this earlier. If you've filled out the Meeting Preparation worksheet (found on my website) and at least skimmed the rest of this book, you're set.

Sleep: Any parent knows how screwed up you are when you're sleep-deprived. You're crabby and mentally dull, neither of which will help you advocate for your child. The night before a meeting is not the time to stay up too late binging a show or doom scrolling.

Healthy Movement: Pick a workout that fits your time and mood, but aim to get at least 5 minutes of movement in. Make sure the dog gets a quick walk in the morning, do a five-minute yoga flow, run with angry music in your ears, or search YouTube for your preferred type of workout. But please, do something, even if it's just parking at the far end of the lot. Not only does exercise release dopamine (AKA the feel-good hormone) into your system, but it also clears your head, allowing your subconscious to process and prepare you for the coming meeting, and it revs your body with the energy needed to get through a stressful situation.

Quiet Time: Most of the practices and techniques covered in Chapter 4 "Establish Your Foundation" count here. The point is to spend a few minutes calming and focusing your mind and body. Focus on how grateful you are for the resources available or the awesome personality your child has, or the solid rock of support you've found in your spouse/mom/friend. Acknowledge that people in education are there because they love teaching children…your child, as a matter of fact. And even if you don't agree with them on everything, approaching them with gratitude for what they do will set a good tone for the meeting to come. You could also spend a few moments visualizing how you want the meeting to go. Focus on how you want to feel (steady, assertive, confident) and see the other side as relaxed, open to your requests, and committed to providing the best for your child.

Fuel: Don't eat garbage in the morning. I know you know this. Don't have more caffeine than you would on a normal day, and get some protein in.

If the meeting is scheduled to last more than 30 minutes, then bring some sort of treat or fuel for the team. One of the key lessons I learned in the military is that if you feed people, they will be happier than they were. And happier troops, ones with either caffeine or sugar in their systems, tend to feel appreciated and want to work harder for and with the provider of said delightful morsels. If I'm heading into an early meeting, I'll email the day before to get everyone's Starbucks order. Afternoon meetings get a pan of brownies or mini chocolate chip cookies. This doesn't have to be expensive (homemade brownies are fine), but it will get you **so much** in return. Trust me.

Feed the Troops! A key lesson I learned in the
military is that fed people are happy people
who feel appreciated. And appreciated people
work harder for and with you. Simple as that.

18

WRITING IEP GOALS

Casting a Vision for the Future

Before you get into the actual IEP meeting where you are setting the goals for your child, I encourage you and your partner/co-parent to pause for a moment. Even if your kiddo is just in preschool, what is your vision for him? What does a full, rich life look like for your child? Put aside practicalities for the moment; technologies and medicine will advance as your child ages, making more things possible for them. And the last thing you want to do is underestimate your child. So, even if you have doubts or uncertainties about the **how**, what are your hopes and dreams for your baby? Think about all the aspects of a full life: What do you want their living situation to be? Who are they spending time with? Do they have a family of their own? What about their finances, career, education, etc.?

As your child gets older, ask them what they see for their future. What are their hopes and dreams? Allow their vision and dream to be as big and audacious and rich as they can imagine. Over the course of their childhood, allow their vision and goals for themselves to take priority over those you have for them. You will also want to periodically refine this overarching vision of your child's life as you learn more and more about who they are, what they want, and their strengths and weaknesses – just as you would for any child as they grow and mature.

In the context of a child with an IEP, this vision becomes the guiding light for setting specific IEP goals. Based on the vision, create a "skill tree" that outlines all the skills required to achieve it. Start with the high-level skills and then drill down into what building-block skills are needed to achieve each of them. Go as many levels down through the skills until you get to the foundational skills needed. Once you have brainstormed what this list might look like, you can work with the IEP team to look at the age and developmentally appropriate milestones for acquiring those skills and see where your child's abilities are lagging. These are the areas that should drive the goals included in the IEP.

Skill Tree Example

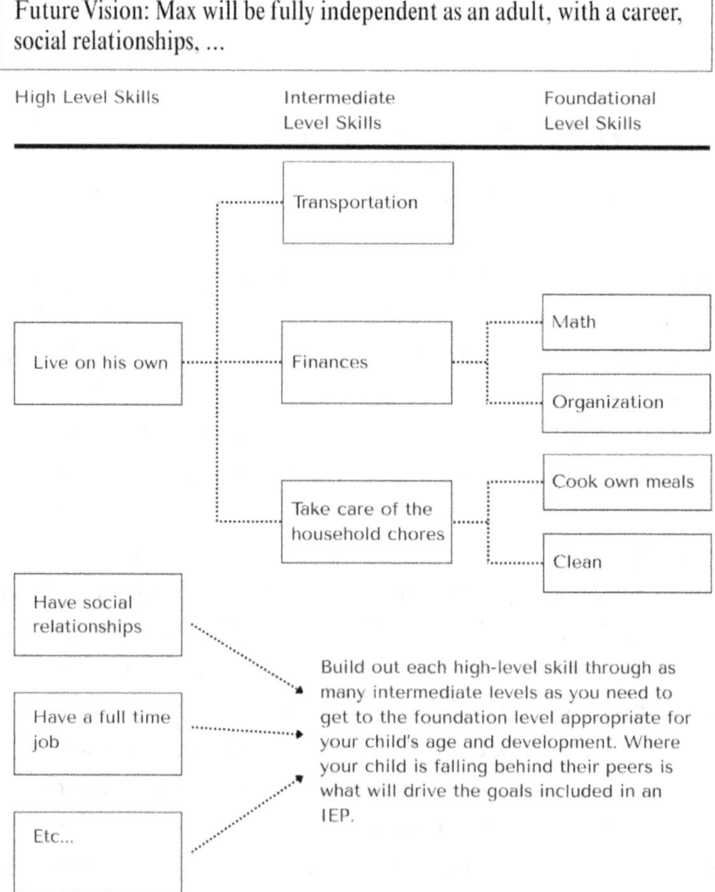

Let's walk through an example here so you can follow the process. My big vision for Max is that he lives fully independently, with a family and career (and hopefully gives me grandchildren one day). As Max has gotten older, the details of how he wants to achieve those goals have changed, but the basic high-level skills he needs remain the same. Broadly, in order to live on his own, he will need to manage his own finances, transportation, social relationships, career, and household.

Focusing on a single high-level skill, such as managing his own finances, we see that it requires competence in reading, math, technology, and organization. Similarly, to handle household management, he must have skills in organization, cooking, cleaning, and home maintenance. Regardless of the career path he selects, essential skills include communication, organization, and reading.

Now, during IEP meetings, because we have shared our vision of Max's future with the overall team for years, together we can take a look at each of these skills and pair them up with age and developmentally appropriate milestones to see where he either meets the expectations or is struggling to learn the skills and is falling behind. Because we have the big picture mapped out, we can start building the actual goals and deciding how to measure progress towards learning the skills needed for his future vision.

I want you to keep this one thing firmly in mind — moving your child towards your vision for them (including your child's input) should be the #1 driver of the IEP goals. Given this, **your input** and **active leadership** during this part of the discussion are critical. Please do not let the school set this vision and roadmap without you, and do not allow the team to rush through writing them. I just want you to remember, the people sitting across the table from you are just about as skilled at writing goals as you are. Yes, they've seen a lot more IEP goals than you likely have; however, their formal training is in education, not goal writing. Speak up and play an active role in writing these goals. If you've worked hard to create a collaborative team so far, then they shouldn't resist any questions or suggestions you make in regards to IEP goals. If they do give you grief here, stay calm, insist on your right to provide input, and escalate if you need to.

Note: I've included some prompts/questions at the end of this chapter to help you walk through the process of moving from the big picture of your vision down to the goals, as well as the high-level skills down to foundational ones needed to achieve them. You can work through it verbally or fill out the blank worksheet (found in the Book Resources page on my website) with your partner before you head into the IEP meeting and discuss this with the whole team.

Writing Goals to Support the Vision

Before we dive into the specifics of writing goals, I just want to point out that it is not your responsibility to write these goals on your own before the IEP meeting. Your job is to hold and communicate the vision of your child's future to the team and ensure the goals proposed by the school support it. The school-based members of the IEP team will come to the meeting with a set of proposed goals written out. Do not let them tell you that you have to accept what's written or that you can't change them. Legally, they must allow you to have input, but don't worry, they aren't going to expect you to show up with goals of your own.

That being said, I want to walk you through the pieces that make up a well-written goal so you know what you're looking for. Is it **relevant** to your child and the vision? Is it **specific** to them and their situation? Is it **achievable** within the **timeframe** proposed? And how will you know if they are achieving it? What and how will the school **measure** their progress towards achieving it?

When writing or evaluating any goal, start with this very basic question: Does it advance our vision for our child? Is it **relevant** for our child this year based on their current skill set? As an example, if we're talking about our goal for Max to be employed and financially independent as an adult, a relevant goal in 6th grade might be to actively participate in class discussions. Now, as a senior, the relevant goal supporting this part of the vision might be to turn all work in on time. Relevant IEP goals should take your child from where she is in her development today to one step closer to achieving her vision.

Each goal should focus on a **specific** skill or behavior that your child needs extra help with to achieve their version of success (the future vision). These goals might be written specifically for your child, or they may come from the school's idea bank/"big book of IEP goals." Ultimately, it doesn't matter as long as it passes the litmus test of relevance to your child and meets their developmental needs. These goals can and should change from year to year as your child grows and her needs change, so don't feel like an IEP goal needs to cover too much ground. Make it specific to the next step that needs to be taken and then adjust it when appropriate.

Building on the foundation we've already set (IEP goals must be relevant and specific to support your child's future vision), we next have to consider what she can reasonably **achieve** within a specific **timeframe**. This timeframe is usually one school year, but there's no rule that says they can't span multiple years of a child's academic career. Goals should include mini progress goals over the course of the year (i.e., William should be doing X 50% of the time by November 15, 60% of the time by February 28, and 80% of the time by May 20). Then define when you'll receive updates on the progress toward the goals. Typically, these mini-goal dates align with the school calendar and fall at the same time as quarterly report cards, parent-teacher conferences, or mid-terms if your children are older. So, using the previous example, William's parents should receive a progress report from the school shortly after November 15, February 28, and May 20.

In making sure that the goals are achievable, there's a balance that needs to be struck among a couple of considerations: How challenging is the skill, and how long do you and the rest of the IEP team think your child will take to learn and demonstrate it? Does the IEP team have a preference or guidance from their district about multi-step/more complex goals that might take more than one year to achieve? Or would they rather have simpler/shorter goals that can be more rapidly achieved? Playing with how the goal is written and the timeframe of when your child is expected to attain competency of the skill will allow the team to find the right balance for your child.

For example, your future vision for your child includes the high-level goal that they can communicate with others. The foundational goal for your child might look wildly different based on their individual challenges. While the general education curriculum may be focused on handwriting skills to build communication, if they have cerebral palsy and physically can't hold a pencil, then handwriting goals are not useful, because they will never be achievable. A better goal for this child might be to learn how to use an electronic communication board/app or how to type using a modified keyboard over the course of the year.

Similarly, expecting a child with dyslexia, who is currently five reading levels behind her peers, to not only catch up, but also make the expected three reading level improvement by the end of the school year (equating to an improvement of eight reading levels in nine months) is probably not realistic either. Breaking it down to improving five reading levels this year and catching up the rest of the way next year gives her a greater chance at success. The point here is to make sure that you've broken big goals down into smaller ones your kiddo can actually achieve.

Okay, you have the vision, and you've worked with the team to develop a goal that is specific, relevant, and achievable within a defined timeframe. Now, the last thing to work through with the team is to make sure that you are **measuring** the right thing to show progress (or lack thereof) toward achieving the goal. Because I know defining the measurement part of a goal can be frustrating, I'd like to take a step back before diving into the nitty-gritty of this section.

It can feel like this is a really important piece to get right, but I want to recenter you on a couple of things. First, remind yourself (and the team if necessary) of what everyone gains by agreeing on both the future vision of your child and how the team will measure his progress towards acquiring the skills he needs. With common expectations established, when members of the team switch out between school years (remember IEPs last for a calendar year, so most span parts of two school years), the transition is smoother, and evaluations are consistent no matter who is taking the measurements/observations. Especially if you don't feel fully supported by the school, a clearly defined measurement approach helps hold the school accountable for teaching the agreed-upon skill(s).

What the measurements don't do, however, is ensure your kiddo actually learns the skill(s) and achieves the goal(s). Measurement, by its nature, is separate from teaching and also learning. While effective measurement will tell you if learning is happening, teaching/learning doesn't need to be measured to be effective. So while yes, measurement is important and a required part of the IEP goal, it doesn't need to be perfect for the **teaching** and **learning** to be effective and for your child to thrive. Do your best here, don't stress over it, and if something feels off as the year progresses, you can always modify the IEP mid-year.

All that being said, let's talk about what effective measurements might look like in your child's IEP. Solidly developed goals will define when the measurements will be taken. They will spell out how often data will be collected and at what time(s) of the day. <u>When</u> can also dictate <u>where</u> measurements are taken. If you are writing a goal about improving behavior in PE, then make sure it states that all data should be collected during PE class. Walk through the process from beginning to end in your mind. How will this information (data) be collected, and what will it look like when it comes back? Will it really tell us what we want to know?

Ideally, you will want to make sure the information you're going to collect is as <u>objective</u> as possible, as opposed to subjective. Objective means that it is free from personal feelings or opinions in representing the facts. Subjective means it depends on someone's opinion — namely, the person giving the score. Examples of subjective measures might be "better behavior" or "improvement in listening." You can still have a goal that achieves "improvement in listening," but you need to tighten it up so it's measurable and hopefully more objective. When we're talking about measuring a child's progress towards learning a skill, true objectivity may be hard to achieve, as so much of it will require a person's observations. It is still worth the effort to incorporate as many objective measures as possible.

For example, for a goal of "improve listening skills," a subjective goal might read, "Aiden will do a better job listening in both the cafeteria and classroom settings." What defines "better" and who gets to decide it? To turn this goal into one with more objectivity, it might read, "Aiden will respond to teacher requests with no more than one reminder, 80% of the time, as measured on random data days during both academic and social settings." This goal now gets you some numbers you can work with and track over time to see if Aiden is moving in the right direction. "Random data days" is language you might see that simply means the days the evaluator for this goal will observe/gather data are random, not predetermined. Most evaluators will attempt to gather data across a variety of situations and environments (e.g., the lunchroom, art, and homeroom), but if this diversity of scenarios is important, write it into the goal.

You've defined <u>what</u> you are going to track and made it as objective as possible, now determine <u>who</u> is going to be taking the sample data and doing the measurements. Having a regular observer will add consistency and reliability to your data. Make sure that the person selected has the capacity to actually provide the data you're requesting. For example, you can't have the general classroom teacher taking an hour's worth of observations, but a para-educator or the special education teacher might be able to sit in the back of the classroom and do just that.

Next, think about <u>how</u> the data is going to be collected. Will you be taking it from test scores? Will it be from observations noted on a standardized data collection sheet? What will the numbers/data look like after you collect them? You will need to pay close attention to the numbers and how the calculations will be done.

You might initially be intimidated by math, but mock up a couple of scenarios and see how the proposed method of data collection and the resulting measurements would play out. Make sure the numbers accurately give you a picture of what's going on; otherwise, you will end up with data that tells you your child has met her goal, while you and the rest of the team know that isn't true.

In one of Henry's IEPs, the goal initially proposed was "Reduce the amount of time Henry spends in a calm-down spot to an average of 20 minutes per class per day." The data was going to be collected from a daily report that was already being used and was broken down into 15 "classes." The proposed calculation was Amount of Time in Calm-Down Spot divided by 15 = Average Amount of Time per class Spent in Calm-Down Spot.

At first glance, I thought, 'Yeah, that would work.' But once I walked through a likely scenario, I could see the goal was flawed. Let's say Henry has an issue right after lunch and goes to his Calm-Down Spot like he's supposed to, but he shuts down and decides not to come back in with the class. He spends the rest of the day there, a total of three hours. Clearly, this isn't in alignment with the goal, right? But, if we do the math for the day, assuming Henry had no other issues, his 180 minutes divided by 15 chunks of time gives us an average of 12 minutes per class spent out of the class. So the data tells us he had a great day and is achieving his goal, but we know his day was about as opposite of success as you can get.

In this instance, the goal was rewritten to be "Reduce the amount of time Henry spends in a calm-down spot to an average of less than 10 minutes per occurrence." The data was measured as the amount of time spent in the calm-down spot each time he went there, and the math was adjusted to look like Total Amount of Time Spent in Calm-Down Spot for each "visit" divided by Number of Times Calm-Down Spot Visited for the period, which gives us the Average Time Spent per visit. This measurement now provides our team with the data needed to identify if he is making progress with the tools he's been given or if something needs to be tweaked.

Writing goals doesn't necessarily come easily to any of us, even for the educators who do this way more than you or me. You'll likely make some mistakes along the way and have to edit some goals, either mid-IEP cycle or during an annual review. Just take your time, hold the future vision, ask a million questions, and remember that the important part is that your child gains the skills they need for a successful life. Everything else is secondary. Even if the goals are poorly written, data doesn't get collected, you miss progress reports, and whatever else might go wrong, **but** your child still learns the skill, then that's a win for your child, for you, and for the entire IEP team.

Prompts to Consider for Goal Creation

- What is your overarching vision for your child's life? Include all aspects: what level of education do they reach, their living situation, finances, employment, social life, etc.
- If your child is old enough, what is **their** vision for their own life? Again, considering all aspects.
- What are the high-level skills necessary for achieving that (combined) vision?
- What skills are necessary as building blocks for those high-level skills? For example, if the high-level skill is cooking for oneself, the building blocks might be the ability to read and follow directions, be safe and focused in the kitchen, planning and creating the grocery list, etc.
- What are the age or developmentally appropriate skills that we can focus on **this year** that build toward the high-level skills necessary to achieve our child's best future?
- How do we know they are making progress toward learning these skills?

19

NEGOTIATION

You should approach every sit-down meeting with the IEP team as a negotiation. I know the word negotiation sounds serious, and many people feel completely anxious when they even hear it. Most go straight to a vision of the used-car salesman or buying a car where there's a serious information and power gap. Try to think of it as a strategic discussion, not an argument, and you'll be in the right frame of mind to accomplish what you need to on behalf of your child. They have something you need, and they control the access to it. But this doesn't mean that the meeting has to have (or should have) a negative tone or be combative. Things are rarely resolved by shouting, and people certainly don't feel better about working together when they've been yelled at, belittled, or bullied into doing something for the other party.

Over my 15+ years as a contract negotiator for some of the largest companies in the world, I've picked up a few tricks and tried-and-true strategies **anyone** can use. I will break them down into what you can do leading up to the meeting/negotiation and how to act when sitting across the table from the school representatives.

Rebe's Rules for Preparing for a Negotiation

One: Listen. Yes, this is important even *before* you get into the room. Listen to what the teacher is telling you about what is and isn't working in the classroom currently. Listen to what other parents have said about their meetings with the school.

Two: Be prepared. If you've been reading from the beginning, you've already got this one solidly in your back pocket. The key to any negotiation is knowledge. Go back and review Chapter 17 "How to Prepare for Meetings" and follow the process I outline there. You must know the details of your side so well that you see it on the backs of your eyelids when you close your eyes. What is the situation with your child? What has the teacher been telling you? What medical opinions have you already sought out? This is where the (physical or digital) notebook you've already pulled together comes in handy. Look at you, Mama! You've already gathered all this information into one spot! Review it, make sure it's up to date and organized.

Three: Know what you really want. This requires some introspection and a bit more research. What are you asking the school to do? What are common services provided to children like yours? Next, you'll need to flesh out two possible scenarios. First, decide what you would like to see provided by the school and call this the Best Possible Outcome. Then, outline the minimum you are willing to accept from the school – this is what's known in a traditional negotiation as your Walk Away Point, but really it's your "I'm gonna fight like hell and appeal all the way to the State Board of Education if needed" point. You will want to aim the conversation towards the best possible outcome, and away from your walk away point if at all possible. Anything that doesn't meet that standard is unacceptable and means you walk away from the table without an agreement and with the intention of appealing. This should be your absolute last resort because this tends to sour a relationship fast. That is definitely not your goal.

Four: Know what the other side wants or needs. What are the constraints on your local school district? Do you know any other children in your school/district with a similar situation? Talk to their parents to get an idea of the supports provided for them, so you know, in general, what the school might offer your child. This is a critical piece of the equation… if you can understand what the school can or can't do and prepare your request accordingly, then you'll position yourself in a much better place to achieve a solution that's pretty darn close to your best possible outcome.

I covered this exercise in "How to Prepare for Meetings," but it's worth repeating here. Take everything you've thought about in the steps above and write down your answers to the following questions:

What are the key topics, goals, or decisions that need to be made in this upcoming meeting? This includes topics that are key to both sides.

How do I feel about each of these items? What would my best-case scenario outcome be for each of them?

What do I believe the school wants for each of these outcomes?

What is the worst-case outcome I'm willing to accept? This is known as your walk-away point, where if you don't get at least this minimum level of whatever, you would shut down the meeting and walk away (most likely in a school setting to appeal to the next higher level in the food chain).

Looking at this list of topics, goals, and decisions, what are my top three, and which ones are less important? Rank them from most to least important **to you,** and then repeat the ranking from the school's perspective.

Looking at this list, where are there holes in the information I have at hand that I could gather before the meeting? Does or will that information change your best-case or worst-case scenarios or your importance ranking of the item?

Here is a worksheet you can use to organize this information, with a sample topic filled out. You can find a blank one at the end of this book, as well as on my website.

Negotiation Outline

Key Topic/ Goal/ Decision to be made	Topic #1 (EXAMPLE) Get Max evaluated for special needs	Topic #2
What is my best-case outcome for this item?	Max gets the full battery of evaluations necessary to figure out what is going on and how to tailor his education and the teaching methods so that we unlock the highest potential he has	
What do I think the school wants to happen here?	The school would rather not provide the resources for expensive evaluations due to a severe state-wide budget crunch. They want to wait until Max is failing before performing evaluations and committing to an IEP and the resources needed to fulfill one.	
What is my minimum acceptable solution? My walk-away point?	The minimum I'm willing to accept is evaluations for ADHD, Speech, and a Learning Disability. I know this is what he needs. I'm willing to fight to guarantee this outcome.	
What rank is this on my priority list?	Number One - nothing is more important.	
Do I need more information on this topic?	I'm not sure what other evaluations are available or are appropriate for the signs we've been seeing in Max.	
Questions to ask about this topic	• What are the other evaluations that would be appropriate to complete at this time to give us the fullest picture of what we're dealing with here and how to best help Max? • What will we learn from each evaluation? • What is the exact name of each evaluation to be performed (so we can Google it later)? • If a specific evaluation is rejected, why? • Etc.	
Outcome	** If you bring this worksheet with you, fill out this block as you go along. One, you'll look so prepared it sends a strong message to the others in the room that you are #uneffwithable. And two, this allows you to recap all the decisions made at the end of the meeting to make sure everyone is on the same page. Win-win!	

Five: Make use of non-verbal ways to establish an equal playing field. One of the easiest ways to set yourself up as an equal member of the team is to look the part. Today is not the day to wander into the school in your yoga pants, even if you are a yoga instructor. When things were rather difficult with my son's first school, my husband and I would walk into meetings in suits with briefcases in hand. We wanted them to have no doubt as to who they were dealing with, but you probably don't need to start at that level. Please note: suits were not out of line for either of our professions, so this was merely one step dressier than I normally went to work. You do **not** need to go buy a suit for this process. You can absolutely achieve this with a nice pair of jeans and a sweater from Walmart. And, as always, adjust my advice to fit your community and culture.

The point here is that you want to match the level of formality of the administrators (who are the decision makers) in this meeting. In doing so, the other members of the IEP team will be more likely to subconsciously see you and then treat you as one of their peers, which lends you more power in influencing decisions, etc., than a "frazzled mom." You want to look polished, professional, and organized — in other words, **confident and ready.**

In addition to the clothes you wear, you will want to look prepared for the meeting. Have your key documentation tidy and ready in a file folder, bring along your physical notebook if you created one, have your Parent Organizer (found in the resources section) for the meeting filled out, and have pen and paper for notes ready. Negotiations are a game, and you have a role to play, complete with a costume and props. I know this "game" has very real and lasting impacts on your child – please believe me, I know. But if you really want to be successful in advocating for your child, you have to know the rules and play by them.

Rebe's Rules of Negotiation

One: Remember you are all part of the same team. Own your part in **setting the tone** before you even start talking. Start with appreciation. This is likely to be a long meeting, and you need them to agree to give you something they have and you want/need for your child. They are taking time out of the classroom (sometimes giving up their precious planning period for the day) and away from providing services to other children to meet with you and discuss your child. Make sure you come in working towards collaboration and cooperation, and presuming good intentions from everyone involved.

Two: Set the tone by taking an active leadership role. Yes, the IEP team has to reach an agreement on the outcome and details of whether and how your child will receive services going forward, but you are the only one there with laser-focused attention on your child. Everyone else in the room is juggling the needs of all the other children in the school or classroom, along with your child's needs. This makes you, not them, the ultimate authority and expert on your child. Be confident that you have a valuable role on the team and that your contributions are critical to your child's success.

Three: Listen. This is so important, I'm going to go over it again. Being quiet enough to listen and absorb is **not** a natural thing to do. Humans are hard-wired, it seems, to want to fill the dead space in a conversation with chatter. Let **them** do the talking and really listen to what they are telling you. This does a couple of things: First, it makes them uncomfortable, so they fill in the silence with chatter. Uncomfortable, anxious people reveal more and "give up" more during a negotiation than the ones who can remain calm, unflustered, and silent. Second, they might offer you more than you were going to ask for on a particular issue. They are responsible for providing services to your child — let them make the first offer. And last, it's just a good communication habit to cultivate. Listening and then repeating what they said back to them in your own words provides everyone with an opportunity to make sure you heard them correctly and are on the same page.

Ask a question and then *hush already* so they can answer. Even after 15 years of practice, this is hard for me — I always want to give three examples and five sentences of explanation to make sure what I said makes sense. But when I can rein myself in and focus on listening instead of talking, I get much better results. For example, if your child is non-verbal, this might look like asking, "What options are available for providing me with daily updates on how the school day went for Bobby?" and then you zip it. Don't rush right into the brainstorming process and toss out the zillion ideas you've already come up with for a daily communication log. Ask your question and then let them answer.

This is a practice, so start today in your day-to-day interactions with everyone you come into contact with. It will be really, really uncomfortable at first, but it will not only make you a better negotiator, but it will also make you a better communicator overall.

Four: Keep Calm. This one can be extremely challenging, but it's probably the single most important thing you can do during an actual negotiation. You can bring bagels, wear a suit, and listen until your ears bleed, but if you start ranting and raving once it's your turn to speak, then you've lost. Plain and simple. And it's not that **you** lost, your child will be the one hurt the most if you lose your temper. You've also just lost the ability to partner with these people and advocate for your child, long-term. Trust me, I've been sorely tempted and have written more angry emails (that I never sent) and said more awful things (in the privacy of my head, or to my husband, who wanted to say the same things at the time) than I can count. But those emotions were **locked down tight** the minute I stepped out of my car in the parking lot. Go back and review Part II "Sanity-Savers" and Chapter 17 "How to Prepare for Meetings" if you need to.

All I can do here is tell you that you need to figure out what works for you and do it. Because I guarantee there will be moments that might make your blood boil or break your heart. You will be triggered. I don't care who you are and what training you've had – when it comes to a meeting about your struggling child, you will get emotional. But, if you allow these emotions to swamp you and you lash out, a couple of things will happen: You'll stop listening, and you'll miss important things in the conversation. You'll alienate the people you need to work with in order to get your child what she needs, which will decrease the amount of extras your child will get. And you'll not only lose this team's cooperation and respect, but word will spread, and you'll encounter greater resistance with next year's IEP team, as well. It's just human nature – people will give more to someone who is nice, and they will grudgingly give the bare minimum if you're a jerk. Don't be a jerk.

Remember, negotiating isn't the same thing as arguing, so keeping your emotions in check will serve you well. You may have seen negotiations portrayed on TV or in movies as tense, drama-filled yelling matches. Not even during my time negotiating in the Air Force did I ever yell or see anyone else yell in a negotiation. Raised voices have happened, and tensions can run high, but these are the things you're trying to avoid. Especially when you're working with someone you need to have a solid relationship with going forward, you don't want the tactics you use here to sour the relationship moving forward.

Five: Take your time. You will probably be surprised by something during one of these meetings. It might be a diagnosis you were/weren't expecting or a decision not going the way you expected. Despite your best efforts, you may get emotional or flustered.

It's okay to ask for a moment to compose yourself. It's okay to ask for a longer break and request a private space to pull yourself together or regroup with your partner to get back on the same page.

It's okay to ask for a meeting to be stopped and rescheduled for a later date. It's okay to not agree to a goal until they provide you with the documentation that supports its inclusion. It's okay to ask questions until you understand the topic at hand. Don't let the school representatives rush through the meeting. Yes, you are in their building, and they might be running the meeting, but you are an equal member of the team. By law (IDEA), they cannot create or make changes to an IEP without your input and approval. Here, you might say, "I think we might all benefit from a small break. Where's the closest restroom I might use?" or "I'm going to need to research that before I agree to anything else. When can we reconvene? I'm available…"

Six: Make them tell you no three times. So what do you do when you've asked for something, and they say no? Especially if this item is on your "I'm going to walk away if they say no to…" list, you ask for it again, but in a different way. You get curious and ask for an explanation for **why** it isn't available in your situation. Is it funding? Is it not appropriate, and why not? Is it just not standard practice, but should be? If you're satisfied with this explanation and are willing to remove it from your walk-away list, then you say okay and move on to the next thing. But if you're not happy with the reasoning you've heard and they're still saying no, then you have a tough decision to make.

If you reach this point and it becomes clear that you will not reach an agreement with the school on a critical point, you may have to end the meeting and appeal the situation. You can approach this in a couple of ways. You could suggest a pause on that particular point and move on to other parts of the meeting. If it's a key decision that affects the rest of the decisions that need to be made (like whether your child will be evaluated), you may have to actually "walk away" and leave the meeting. If you think you just need a break to consider options, schedule the next meeting to regroup as a team before you leave. However, you might need to end the meeting and then escalate your conflict/concerns to the next level within the school's hierarchy. This might look like you respectfully saying, *"I disagree with your decision to not include speech therapy for Trevor, but I don't want this to derail the whole meeting. Can we move on to the next items?"* or *"I understand you've made your decision. I will be appealing it."*

The goal of each meeting is to make some sort of decision, and you must use every tool you can to influence that decision. However, every meeting is also a chance to build and strengthen the relationship you have with the school and the individuals who will directly support your child. You can do both if you stay focused on team building, remain calm and positive, walk in prepared, ask for what is in the best interest of your child, know where you can compromise, and avoid issuing ultimatums.

20

HOW TO ACT
WHEN IT'S GOOD

WHEN IT'S GOOD, life is easy. Everyone on the team is in agreement with the plan, the kids are behaving, teachers are teaching, birds are singing... you get the picture.

In all seriousness, though, even when it's all good, you've got work to do. **Now** is the time to work on building those strong relationships with your team. Show appreciation as often as you can, either via a handwritten note of thanks or with a random gift of treats you whipped up over the weekend. Regardless of what you decide to do, make sure you're using this gift of time you've been given to strengthen the relationships you will absolutely need to rely on when/if something happens, and it all goes sideways.

This is also a time to consider paying it forward by reaching out to other special needs families in your school and community. If you find yourself with an extra bit of capacity, ask yourself, "How can my talents make this road easier for someone else?" This doesn't have to be a huge time commitment. I completely understand what you're thinking. Just because things are going well doesn't mean there aren't a **million** things still to do for your own family. Just remember how lost you felt when you started looking for a book like this one...there are so many other mamas a few steps behind you on the path. Consider doing what you can to light a lantern or two for them, okay?

Things to do when it's good:

- Build positive relationships with classroom and special education teachers
- Show appreciation to your team
- Get organized
- Get caught up on filing at home
- Volunteer at the school
- Volunteer in the community
- Light Lanterns for others

21

HOW TO ACT
WHEN IT'S BAD

WHAT DO YOU DO WHEN YOU hit a bump in the road? When the team doesn't agree, or something changes unexpectedly with your kiddo and you guys are scrambling to adjust or find a solution ASAP, what do you do? How do you act?

When Henry was in crisis, and his behavior was so unpredictable that he was almost expelled from school, things were bad. I had no idea what was wrong with him, and I was desperate for answers and support. I needed **immediate help**, dammit, and one thing that does not move fast is any part of this process. It takes forever to get in with pediatric specialists. It was late in the school year, and he was in preschool, so getting the early childhood team mobilized was looking like a long shot. But my baby was deteriorating right before my eyes, and there wasn't anything I could do in the moment to help him. I developed anxiety and panicked every time my phone rang because I never knew if it was the school saying he'd hurt someone else or trashed another classroom and needed to come home. I said I'm sorry to others more times than I can count. And I cried. Oh, I cried. I cried buckets of sad tears, scared tears, tears of frustration and exhaustion, and so many oh-my-god-I'm-not-strong-enough-to-do-this-one-more-minute tears.

So how did I choose to behave during my darkest hours as a parent?

How did I interact with others when my back was against the ropes, and I was getting pummeled?

How I Acted Towards Myself

I chose to prioritize my self-care, using the tools and practices from Part II. I knew I couldn't be of any use to my kids if I let myself get run down. I dialed in my nutrition, movement, and rest to make sure my body was taken care of, and got serious about meditation to help my spirit find some precious moments of peace.

I chose to be picky about what went on my to-do list. I knew something had to give, so I decided to say no to things. I decided to put some things on the back burner, to flat-out ignore others, and to hire help when and where I could afford it. (I'll be honest, a good housekeeper is a non-negotiable expense for me, and I won't pretend otherwise.)

I chose to ask for help. I got myself into therapy and support groups. I leaned hard on the family I'm so blessed to have living close to me. I also stopped worrying about eating out, using paper plates, or anything else that made life just a tiny bit easier during that season.

How Did I Act Toward Others?

I chose to take a deep breath before opening my mouth. I knew I had to be centered and think for a hot minute before I said anything. I knew going in, yelling and screaming would close way more doors in my face than it would open.

I chose to be clear and kind in my communication with others. This isn't the same as being "nice." "Nice" is not kind if it's dishonest. "Nice" doesn't allow all parties to get their needs met because it's performative. Clear and kind communication, though, provides a way for you to express your or your child's needs explicitly. (See Chapter 15 "Communication" for more.)

I chose to lead with gratitude, thanking people for their help even before they gave it. This works especially well when dealing with the scheduler at the doctor's office or any other "gatekeeper," such as the school secretary. I know it's hard to hear that the next appointment is in six months, but if you can make the other person feel genuinely appreciated, they might make the extra effort to try to squeeze your child in earlier. Even if it doesn't benefit you directly, if you've spent even a single shift in customer service, you know how it feels to be treated poorly. I try to take every opportunity to ensure that the people I interact with feel seen and appreciated.

I chose to use humor, even when it was a little soggy from the tears leaking through. I knew people would respond better to someone who they could tell was doing their best to make some damn lemonade out of a tough situation.

But really, how did I act when I realized we'd been misled into thinking our son didn't need an IEP? When I realized the school was oh-so-very wrong?

I chose to do all the things I've just written about here in this book. I chose to be an active member of the IEP team. I knew that if I didn't speak up, they would arrange things to suit their goals, not in a way that would prioritize my son's needs.

I chose to get smart. I knew I needed to know my child's rights better than the school district did. I did a lot of homework and contacted an advocate immediately so I could fix a process that had gone sideways on us. I spent many a lunch hour reading anything I could find so I could call the school on their lies from a position of knowledge and power.

I chose to get serious about documentation. I knew I needed proof of everything to ensure we got what we needed and they couldn't pull a fast one on us again.

I chose to bring my A-game to every meeting, from taking care of myself to feeding the crew; I pulled out all the stops.

I chose to remember exactly who was causing the problem (at our first school, it was the principal). I knew who was throwing up the roadblocks and made sure I didn't take it out on innocent bystanders, like the teacher, social worker, or therapists (or my family).

I chose to keep a tight rein on my tone of voice and choice of words. I knew if I slipped up, I would be handing them ammunition to use against me.

I chose to take my time before agreeing to anything. I knew I had the right to take at least a day to read and review any document they pushed at me.

I chose to ask a million questions and then double-check any answers I received. I knew asking questions would not make me look weak. I also knew I'd been misled in the past, so any answer was taken with a grain of salt and then fact-checked to the best of my ability, at my earliest convenience.

PART V

PRACTICAL AND SUSTAINABLE SELF-CARE

SO MUCH OF YOUR FOCUS has been sucked up by getting your kiddo support that you probably feel consumed by it, right? As parents, we feel keenly the burden of resolving problems, especially medical or school issues. It's a scary, foreign world you've been suddenly thrust into, and most of us go straight to survival mode.

Do you know who suffers most when you're in survival mode? **You do.**

Do you know who suffers next when you're tapped out? **Your family and kids.**

The very ones you're fighting **for** are the ones who lose out when you've got nothing left to give. So let's talk very seriously about how you're taking care of yourself, Mama.

In Part II "Sanity-Savers," I covered quite a bit about things you can do to care for your body, mind, and energy in the moment. And it's true that doing those things over time will compound into measurable changes in your life. But you will likely find that you need to make some **systemic** changes as you settle into this new normal for your family. Parenting not one, but two, special needs children for more than the last decade gives me fairly intimate knowledge of the ebbs and flows this particular situation brings into a person's life, career, and marriage. I know you stand at the sink, washing the dishes while tears run down your face. I know you flinch every time your phone rings or an email dings because you never know if it's the school calling to tell you that your child needs to be picked up. I know you somehow kept it together long enough to help your kiddo through their latest episode, but then you locked yourself in the bathroom/closet/pantry and could only allow yourself five minutes to fall completely apart before wiping off your face, blowing your nose, and faking a smile as you reemerge to help with homework and fix dinner. I know because I've been there, whispering "I'm not strong enough. Oh God, help me. I'm not strong enough," into the soapy dish water.

22

DO IT, DELEGATE IT, DELETE IT

There are as many different definitions of self-care as there are books on my bookshelf, but for me, what helped in the darkest hours fell into three categories: things you can do for yourself, things you need to ask for help with, and tasks to outsource or straight up delete from the list.

Things You Can Do Yourself

This can be broken down into several categories: self-care that takes only a moment; nurturing that requires more time; freebies and cheapies; and expensive splurges. I've included a (nowhere close to comprehensive) list at the end of this section, but the most important thing here is to realize you need to take a minute for yourself before you snap. Then step back and choose from your self-care toolkit based on what the situation allows. Go ahead and make an actual list for yourself before you're totally depleted. Write down small actions that will help you stay calm in the moment, as well as options for when you have a longer stretch of time you can claim.

Whatever you do, please don't let yourself fall into the trap of calling "peeing alone" self-care. You deserve to use your energy for yourself first, not last. I recognize that there are times when you've truly landed in survival mode, and even the concept of self-care flies out the window. But as someone who has been there with my kids and in caring for my aging family members, you cannot allow yourself to operate long-term with zero attention given to your needs. Yes, there will be seasons where the balance will shift and more energy goes out than comes in, but even on the darkest days, you deserve to care for your basic human needs at the very least.

---

*One of the things I like to say to my coaching clients is that I want them to throw out the phrase "you can't pour from an empty cup." I don't want you pouring from your cup at all! It's **your** cup.*

You get to use that energy. Fill your cup so much that it overflows, then that's what you use to give to others. No more of this fill up your cup just so you can drain it for others and never use any for yourself crap. No, ma'am. Never again.

Personally, as an introvert (someone who gets reenergized by quiet, alone time), I'm a huge fan of the "Mommy Time-Out." When I feel like my buttons are being pushed, and I'm one hot second away from losing my cool with the kids, I will tell my boys that I am taking a "Mommy Time-Out." Not only am I using language they can understand by calling it a time-out, but I'm modeling the same critical self-regulation and self-care skills I want them to develop. They see me stepping back and pulling myself together before responding, and it makes it less of a punishment in their eyes when I ask them to take one themselves. I remember the first time I told Max, who was about five at the time, that I was taking a 10 minute Mommy Time-Out. His eyes got huge as he realized the situation must be pretty bad if Mom needs to step away to cool off. And because he understood that I truly needed to step away, he gave me 10 minutes of peace without interrupting, which was huge for him (and me!). Ever since then, I give myself a time-out whenever I know I need to stop and rethink what I'm about to say or do or when I just need to recharge when the kids are around.

Need help brainstorming some more options? Practice some if-then planning. If my child is having a meltdown in public…then I will put them into the car and take 10 seconds for one deep cleansing breath (five-second inhale through the nose, then a five-second exhale through the mouth) before I get in with them. If I'm at the end of a really long stretch of being the rock in the family…then I will carve out a morning just for myself. I will take a bath and indulge in reading a book or watching a favorite movie. If I can afford it, I will treat myself to a facial <u>and</u> a massage, back-to-back at the fanciest spa around.

<table>
<tr><td>Free Self-Care Ideas</td></tr>
</table>

- Take a Mommy Time-Out
- Schedule some time for your favorite hobby
- Read something just for fun
- Start a Gratitude Journal
- Take a hot bath or long shower – make it a luxe ritual
- Spend time with your pets
- Use a meditation app like Headspace, Calm, or Finch (or download the free meditations available on my website *www.rebegoebel.com/bookresources)*
- Take a walk/run/workout to a free video on YouTube (or one of the dusty DVDs you know are in your basement)
- Call or get together with someone supportive
- Get outside and sit in the sun

<table>
<tr><td>Low-Cost Self-Care Ideas</td></tr>
</table>

- Get take out for dinner
- Buy yourself flowers
- Use paper plates
- Go out to eat all by yourself with a book
- Buy yourself a fancy coffee or smoothie
- Splurge on a new nail polish or lipstick
- Take a yoga class – bonus points for doing it with a friend
- Meet up with a friend for lunch, even if it's BYO at the park
- Pay for "no ads" on your favorite app

<table>
<tr><td>Worth Every Penny</td></tr>
</table>

- Hire a housekeeper twice a month
- Get a massage/mani-pedi/facial
- Date Night
- Solo overnight in a hotel, complete with room service
- Lunch at a nice restaurant with a friend
- Noise-cancelling headphones

Things You Need to Ask for Help With

These include tasks that would normally be part of your responsibilities, but due to the extraordinary (hopefully temporary) circumstances you're in, you just can't handle them right now. This could be asking extended family or supportive friends to pick up or watch your other children while you and your spouse are with your kiddo at a doctor's appointment. It could be seeing if your in-laws will cook dinner every Tuesday after Sally's weekly physical therapy appointment across town. It could be asking older children (middle school and up) to take on an extra age-appropriate chore.

I also put stepping back from non-essential commitments in this category. Now is not the time to be leading the women's retreat, chairing the local Humane Society fundraiser, or getting a new puppy (or anything else). Yes, they are all worthwhile activities, but now is the wrong time to be committed to "extra-curricular" organizations. For a time, you will be consumed by figuring out the new normal, and you will be relieved **not** to have 15 more things on your list. This season of your life is temporary, and you will have time and capacity to get involved again, I promise. But not in the beginning. Step away before you let things slip and give yourself something more to worry about as you let other people down.

Tasks to Outsource or Delete

Housework is the first thing to go (in my opinion) if you can afford it. Laundry and grocery shopping tie for a close second on my list because I dread doing both. The only thing I currently hire out is house cleaning, and I swear my housekeeper is the best monthly investment I make. I personally **hate** cleaning, but there is something so very wonderful about having a clean house. It is so indulgently relaxing to have it done for me and the three hours it takes her would take me at least six, and I'd be angry the whole time. So, I skip the drama and look forward to housekeeper days. Boom. No brainer.

To figure out which would be the best tasks for you personally to outsource, make a list of the tasks that have to be done on a weekly/bi-weekly basis. Put a star next to the ones that truly can only be completed by you. These are yours to continue.

Next, check in with yourself on the expectations, or subconscious story, you have around certain tasks. Who told you that things have to be done a certain way, or done at all? Are there things that you're doing, spending your precious time and energy on, that you really don't care about? Stop doing them. It can really be as simple as that.

Seriously, cross off anything that you put on the list but is actually just something Pinterest/the Internet/your judgey Aunt Millie makes you think you should be doing, but isn't really a must-do (decorating for St. Patrick's Day and sorting the Legos by color…I'm looking at you).

Let's take making your bed as an example. Maybe you were raised in a house where you were required to make your bed with an old-school bedspread, pillows in matching shams that you don't actually sleep on, and hospital corners for the sheets. And so that's how you're still making your bed in your house, because that's "just how it's done" or because if your mom stopped by and saw you hadn't made your bed, she'd say something. Okay. Do you actually care if your bed is made that way? Do you **like** making your bed that way? If you like it to look tidy, would you be just as okay with everything just pulled up and smoothed, but no bedspread, frou-frou pillows, and screw the tucked-in sheets? Do you find that you actually don't give a crap about having a made-up bed? Then stop. And just close the door if your mom comes over, because screw anyone for making you feel bad when you're barely treading water.

Now, you should be left with some tasks you can delegate to others and a few you can outsource. Pick the one you hate doing the most and check in with your budget. If you can swing it, make some calls today and start the outsourcing process!

23

WAYS TO STAY POSITIVELY CONNECTED TO FAMILY, FRIENDS, AND COMMUNITY

Stay Connected to Your Partner

One of the key things my husband and I have done that helped tremendously is that we continued to prioritize each other and our relationship during all the madness. No matter what was going on with diagnoses, IEPs, schools, and/or doctors, we tried our best to carve out time away from the kids. You will both need this to stay sane long term, trust me.

When we lived far from family, we made sure to include babysitter costs in the budget each month. Or if my husband was working from home, we would grab lunch together (I worked close to our house…he did not) while the kids were still in school or daycare. Now that I work for myself, I try to meet him close to his office once a week for lunch. I love these lunches because we both have good energy levels mid-day. It's not about being romantic, so no topic is off limits (as long as it's safe to have in public!), and they tend to be cheaper (no babysitter, plus lunch menu, plus no booze, equals a cheap date).

Regardless of the time of day or the activity we chose, having routine opportunities to check in with my husband made a huge difference. We would take the chance to talk about all the things that need to be said but you don't want little ears to hear — like frustrations with the school/teacher/doctor, money concerns, issues with or about the kids themselves, and how to be a united front in responding to certain behaviors. We also talk about things besides the kids, like sharing details about work and other interests…you know, like regular couples do! We just found that when so much of our energy was consumed by caring for children with extra needs, most of the conversations that needed to happen weren't happening. Once we started carving out time to connect and have these discussions, our communication drastically improved. Consequently, I felt significantly more grounded and relaxed knowing that even if everything else was a total disaster, our relationship was solid.

Dealing with all the extra stuff that comes along with having special needs kids can either drive a huge wedge between you and your partner, or it can bring you together as a high-functioning team. Becoming a team requires time and effort, but not nearly as much as doing it all on your own. So do yourself a favor and make sure that you are each on the other's priority list.

Stay Connected to Your Other Children

While there are periods when every child will need more than a sibling might (i.e., a newborn vs. a preschool-aged older sibling), there are special considerations to keep in mind if you have children with special needs. It can be very easy to expect more from the developmentally typical child, especially if they are older. I know I put a lot of pressure on Max to tiptoe around during the year Henry really struggled with autistic meltdowns. I'd ask him to give in to Henry's demands, to do his chores for him, to not do this or say that. I was putting at least part of the responsibility of avoiding a meltdown onto Max's shoulders, and he was only seven. In other families, where a child has more physical needs, I know older siblings have had to learn at a very young age how to hook up a feeding tube, or they suddenly become responsible for cooking dinner every night at the age of ten.

I'm not saying your other children shouldn't be expected to help out. My boys both have chores and help prepare one meal a week now that they're in high school. That's not my point. What I'm trying to get across is that it's easy to not only overlook the child who is developmentally "typical," but it's also easy for expectations to creep in that can make your other children feel resentful and taken advantage of. Please don't lose sight of their needs, even though they might be quieter or less obvious than your child with special needs.

My favorite way to stay connected is to carve out time to spend one-on-one with each of your children to give them your undivided attention. You can make it a monthly routine to have a date with Mom and encourage your partner to do the same. This way, they understand that even if the day-to-day is tough, with most of your attention on the child with special needs, they are still a priority for you. Let them choose the activity or destination, and give them time to talk about how the situation with their sibling makes them feel. You can share age-appropriate details about what's going on and ask for their input on how to solve any issues they bring to you. Let them know you see them and understand how they feel. Or let this be a bubble where it's all about them—follow your child's lead here.

Note that, just like self-care doesn't have to cost a thing to make a big difference, spending time with your children doesn't have to be about spending a ton of money. Trips to the library, bike rides, or even a backyard picnic are great ways to connect with younger children. Now that my boys are teens, our time to connect looks like hopping into the car when my oldest wants to go for a drive, getting ice cream, playing a video game with them, building a fire in our fire pit and sitting on our porch swing, or simply sending each other cute puppy videos on social media. If you take the time to notice where they are asking for your connection and seize every opportunity you can, you'll keep your relationship with all your children strong.

Stay Connected to Your Community

I know just how tempting it is to make your world really, really small, especially at the beginning of this journey. You've hit survival mode, you're overwhelmed with your own situation, and you don't want to be a burden to others. It's also really hard when you realize that **no one** besides other special needs parents understands what you're going through. There's a special brand of (unreasonable, but very real) rage that bubbles up when you hear another parent complain about their kid not making a competitive team, and you're over here just hoping your child doesn't have a seizure today, can figure out how to make friends, or ever live independently. Each parent has valid concerns, but man, it's hard to be gracious sometimes when your concerns feel so much more…everything.

So you might feel like cutting yourself off from your community is the right thing to do. There are seasons of your journey when making your life simple and small is a valid survival strategy. But over the long term, I want to gently encourage you to stay connected to your community.

Staying connected to your friends and other parts of your community will help remind you that you are more than a parent of a child with special needs. That label can become all-consuming, turning into your whole personality if you let it. This is unhealthy for both you and your child(ren). You need activities and other people that light you up, and your kiddo needs you to role-model what adult friendships look like. They need to see that parents are multifaceted human beings who get their needs fulfilled by having many different types of relationships. And *you* deserve to get your needs fulfilled by having many different types of relationships.

Lean on your community for support. Let the people closest to you know that you're struggling and allow yourself to ask for what you need. When we were in the thick of our fight over getting Max tested, none of my closest friends had children yet. But they were so important and helpful in their own ways, from offering to babysit to being a sounding board to taking their lunch hour to listen in on a meeting and take notes for us. Leaning on my friends meant that I was able to spread the "burden" of my fears and anger and worries, and not dump it all on my husband, who was right there with me in his own stew of concerns and frustrations.

You can find support from personal relationships within your community, and also tap into the vast network of connections they may have and the organizations they know about in your region, which exist to support families just like yours and mine. I was never shy about talking about what I was going through with Max. Through those conversations, a friend connected me to one of her friends who was an educational advocate, who got me reading the right books, which shed light on this twisty, dark path — and here I am, a decade later, writing this book. Right after we moved and I was building a new community here in St. Louis, I was again connected through a friend of a friend who told me about an organization that would evaluate Henry for free. Normally, wait times for these evaluations, no matter where you go, are dishearteningly long, but I called right after someone had canceled their appointment, and we were able to get him in later that week. Leaning on my community and asking for their recommendations changed everything for my family in months instead of years.

Raising a child requires the support of a village. Full stop. Adding in the extra complexities and concerns of having a child with special needs makes the village that much more critical to the long-term health of every member in your family. Resist the urge to become insular and stay connected to your community.

24

GET CONNECTED WITH PROFESSIONAL SUPPORT

How to Find a Therapist

Over the course of this book, I've put a lot of responsibility on your shoulders. I know. Some of it can't be avoided or delegated, sorry. However, you may find that there are simply some things you, your partner, and/or your child will need impartial support and specialized skills, tools, or methodologies to work through. A therapist with experience helping people in situations similar to yours will be worth their weight in gold. I simply can't overstate the benefits of finding the right professionals for your support team.

You may be thinking, "I have no idea where to start, and the whole idea makes me uncomfortable." I completely understand! Even though I'm naturally a "talk it out" kinda girl, and not much is off limits once you're in my inner circle, I was still very intimidated by the process of finding a therapist. I didn't know what it would feel like, what to expect, or even how to find a "good" one. Then, given that you're already overwhelmed when you decide you need help with the overwhelm…well, adding another task that isn't cut and dry can feel like the last thing you're capable of doing. This is why I urge you to be proactive about finding therapists for yourself, your partner, and your child before you are in full-blown crisis mode. Seeking someone early affords you more options in the long run.

Depending on your situation, you may want to seek therapy as a family, as other siblings may also benefit from an impartial third party. I know in our family, Max really struggled when all our attention turned to Henry, both because of the sudden shift in focus away from him and because we never knew what would set Henry off into an uncontrollable rage. We were all walking around on eggshells, scared of upsetting him. It took a toll on all of us, and Max benefited greatly from having someone impartial to talk to about the situation. Even if your child has physical (not mental) health issues, therapy can help their siblings. Your other children will need someplace to work through their fears, frustrations, grief, and anger without feeling like they are adding to the burden they know you're already bearing.

Kids see and hear everything and aren't yet developmentally equipped to understand why "bad" things are happening to them or their family. We have dear friends who lost their younger son in an accident. Their oldest went to therapy once, but after seeing his therapist understandably have an emotional reaction herself to his grief, he refused to go back. He doesn't want his pain to inflict pain on others, so he bottles it up. Yes, he absolutely needs therapy. They're working on it. And yes, this child is assuming responsibility for things he logically shouldn't, but developmentally, young children don't yet have the skills to grasp what is their fault and what isn't. The other children in your home may be experiencing something similar, even in a less extreme situation.

Let me explain what you can expect from the process of finding a mental health professional and why you want to have time on your side before I dive into the actual steps you'll need to take to find one.

Finding a therapist is a lot like dating — you may have to sort through some duds before you find someone you click with, and feel comfortable seeing long-term. The first session (or two) with a new therapist will be very one-sided. You'll feel like you just verbally vomited all over this poor person and will walk away without much of a sense of whether you liked them or if they will be helpful. You may temporarily feel worse after talking about all the things that brought you to therapy. But these initial sessions are necessary to bring this total stranger up to speed, and somewhere during the second or third session, you should start to get a glimpse of who this person is as a professional and whether it's worth seeing them for a while. I used to think it took longer, but I've realized after seeing three different therapists myself and four for my children that the gut feel I get early on should be trusted and not to waste additional time before moving on to a new practice.

During your therapy sessions, you'll be able to talk about anything that's on your mind and ask for advice on how to handle certain situations. Every therapist has their own method, which is a unique compilation of all the work they've done, books read, seminars attended, etc. You may be asked to do a homework assignment of some sort between visits and to come back ready to discuss your thoughts on the topic at hand.

For young children, therapy will be largely play-based and will vary widely depending on the needs of your kiddo. We've seen therapists where I was present the whole time and involved in the game play, and others where I was in the room for a family check-in, but then stepped out to the waiting room to give the therapist a chance to speak privately with my child. I've seen some instances where, for really little kids, the parents give the appearance of stepping out, but can watch and listen through a two-way mirror or baby monitor to give you peace of mind about having your child behind a closed door with a relative stranger. You will have to think about what type of situations your child feels most comfortable in and develop a list of questions you can ask any prospective therapists prior to the first meeting.

So if you've never gone to a therapist before, where do you start looking for one? There are two parts to this answer – first, how I think about finding someone, and second, the actual steps you need to take to get this ball rolling.

My thought process generally goes like this: Get recommendations from friends, read reviews, read their bios online, call and ask some questions, set up an initial meeting, go through a couple more sessions, decide whether I do or don't like them, and then either move on to the next option or stick with them for a while. In reality, these steps take a number of weeks or months and aren't that easy, but the payoff is worth the effort. I always start with recommendations and reviews, for basically everything. If I have friends who are in a similar situation, I'll ask them if they're seeing anyone or can recommend anyone to me. I've also asked my primary care doctor, the children's pediatrician, and school counselors or school psychologists. Then I Google the individuals, and read both their bio and any reviews I can find, paying particular attention to any specialties listed as well as accepted insurance providers.

You can also check with your insurance provider for a list of therapists in your area who are in your network. I've always tried to start with someone in network, but sometimes we've had to see someone who is what's called "private pay," meaning they don't accept any insurance plans, and you are 100% responsible for paying their fee in cash or on your credit card. You can, of course, use an HSA/FSA spending account.

You are the only one who can do the math required to decide if you must stay in your insurance network or if your budget allows for private pay. Sometimes, how soon someone can get you in plays just as much of a factor as cost. When Henry was really struggling, I would have sold plasma if I had needed to; time was of critical importance to us. While we all want the best for our kiddos, you also probably don't need the regional expert in XYZ. Sometimes, good enough is a great starting point. You can always switch providers later.

Once I have a list of two or three potential providers, I come up with my list of questions to ask during the initial phone call. Some of my questions include:

- Are you accepting new patients?
- Are you in-network for my insurance plan?
- What is your cancellation policy? (I always remind them that I'm the primary caregiver for small children, and they don't always give me a 24-hour heads up that they're going to get sick.)
- Do you have previous experience in helping people through…?
- How do you structure your visits with minor children?
- How far out are you currently scheduled?
- Do you have after-school or weekend appointments available?
- And so on…

After I've got that pulled together, I sit down to make a bunch of phone calls. Depending on the office situation for the therapist you call, you will either get to talk to a receptionist or you'll have to leave them a message, as they will likely be in with a patient at that moment. If a receptionist answers, you'll be able to ask them the basic questions you've pulled together and decide to either ask for the therapist to call you back or go ahead and schedule your first visit right away.

Even if you think you'll be calling around to other therapists, I always tell people to make the appointment. You can always cancel it later, but this ensures you have one on the books somewhere. Just as with the other specialists you and your children might see, wait times for new patients can be excruciatingly long. I waited over nine months just to be able to **schedule** a new patient appointment with a large pediatric psychiatry group — the first appointment would have been over a year after my initial call. I'm so glad I continued calling around and was able to make an appointment elsewhere! It made the four-week wait we experienced seem like nothing compared to the thought of a full year with no help for Henry. Always take the first available appointment and then ask to be placed on the cancellation list in case something becomes available sooner.

Okay, so now you're sitting in the waiting room, about to walk into your first appointment — what should you expect? During the first two to three sessions, the therapist will want a bit of background on who you are, what brought you to seek therapy, and who the major players in your life are, and so forth. As I've mentioned, I rarely have a problem talking to people, and by the time I'm sitting on that couch, I have a load I need to get off my chest. Just know you'll likely feel worse after dredging everything up during these first visits. There won't be a lot of "therapy" happening — meaning the therapist is still likely trying to get a sense of the situation and your needs before offering suggestions or assigning homework.

During the third visit is when it starts to feel more like a two-way street with you getting input from the therapist. This is where you will have to start thinking about whether you like their style, just like dating. Is this someone you want to continue to invest in? Are you benefiting from them and their methods, or are you not clicking? The first therapist I called in Chicago turned out to be a winner. We had a lot in common, and she felt more like talking to a wiser, more experienced friend than a "therapist." I only stopped seeing her because we moved; otherwise, I would still be her patient. After moving to St. Louis, finding a new therapist took me a couple of tries. The first one I visited about eight times over five months, right when things were really stressful with Henry. I probably should have known we weren't going to click in the first meeting, but I stuck with her until the crisis had passed, and I didn't **need** to work with anyone on a consistent basis anymore.

When I felt I needed to see someone again, I asked around for more recommendations, including from my son's therapist, to see if she had any professional connections she could point me toward. I looked up the one suggested, and after reading a few very positive reviews, I reached out to her. In just two sessions with Dr. B., I felt better about some issues that had been bothering me for over a decade. I knew, when I walked out of that second session feeling lighter and more at peace than I had been in years (about this particular topic), that I had found a keeper. Over time, our relationship ran its course, too, and I stopped seeing her.

Since then, I spent about a year seeing a third therapist to sort through some issues around caring for my parents and the grief of losing my dad to Alzheimer's in 2021 during the height of the pandemic. She was lovely and helped me set some necessary boundaries with other family members, and helped answer some burning "Am I the asshole?" questions. For this therapist, I had looked for someone with specific life experiences, so I knew she would understand me on a deeper level. Again, I was able to resolve the issues that pushed me back into therapy, and our time together came to a natural conclusion. You may find that you benefit from a longer term, routine standing appointment, instead of dipping in and out as I did. Experiment with both strategies, and see what works best for you, then stick with it.

The moral of the story here is that you need to give a therapist some time (more than three sessions) to get to know you and start providing value. But don't stick with a relationship that isn't giving you what you need because you feel awkward about moving on. There are a ton of therapists and social workers out there — you will find the right one if you look and don't settle.

How to Find Non-Traditional, or Somatic, Practitioners

Before I move on, I do want to mention a "non-traditional" type of provider that has truly been instrumental in my growth and healing journey: working with a life coach trained in somatics. Somatic work is an umbrella term for methods that focus on the "soma" or body. Most of what I covered in Part II "Sanity-Savers" falls under this category of work. Therapy can be viewed as a top-down approach: "I don't feel good, so let me see if I can think different thoughts and maybe that will change how I feel." Somatic work is a bottom-up approach: "I don't feel good, so let me change how I feel in my body, which will then give me the capacity to think different thoughts."

Somatic work encompasses breathwork, somatic experiencing, visualization, dance, shaking, vagal toning, sound healing, and a lot more. The more research that emerges about how trauma is stored in the body at a cellular level and can change the expression of our DNA, the more important understanding and incorporating these somatic practices into your self-care will become. We, as a society, tend to treat ourselves as two distinct parts, a body and a brain, and Western medicine follows that thinking. Your medical professional probably only gives surface-level lip service to your mental health, and most therapists never stop to ask how and where you're feeling your guilt/grief/anxiety in your body.

The truth is, we are one. Working to integrate body and mind will yield much greater results than working on them each separately. If you remember back to the beginning of this book, I mentioned that I am personally trained in a variety of movement and breathwork techniques and have been working with my own somatic coach for five years. I use these practices routinely and love how beautifully they can complement traditional therapy methods or stand on their own. Especially if you are working through your own issues on top of supporting your kiddo with special needs, you may want to experiment with finding a somatic practitioner to guide you.

In looking for a somatic practitioner, I would encourage you to start by asking your network of friends and family for recommendations. As the field of somatics is not regulated (yet) by any state licensing oversight, it can be hard to find providers in your area. Word of mouth or checking with local yoga studios, functional medicine providers, chiropractors, wellness centers, and others who lean more towards the "wellness" industry versus "medical" will likely yield a few names for you to research. Don't limit yourself to your local area, either. Even though these practices are body-based, most don't require hands-on work, so you can meet with them virtually and still reap the benefits. My coach isn't even US-based!

Once you start researching someone, I highly encourage you to check out any podcast episodes they may have been on or enroll in a group session/offering they might have coming up. This allows you to get on their newsletter, start getting a feel for how they approach client work, and test them out before you commit to a series of appointments.

Many practitioners will also offer a free "discovery call" where you can chat for a few minutes, ask any questions you may have, and see how they work one-on-one.

Given that somatic work falls under the non-traditional category of care, unfortunately, you won't be able to use your insurance benefits to pay for it. Some may go through and get qualified so you can use your HSA/FSA accounts to pay for them; however, 99% of practitioners will be private-pay only.

I cannot emphasize enough how much somatic work has truly changed my life. While therapy helped me work through some tricky situations, it never helped me **feel** better in my body. Through breathwork and somatic experiencing, I have truly changed my nervous system for the better. The ripple effect has improved every aspect of my relationship with myself and my relationships with my partner, children, other family, and friends.

25

WHEN FAMILY OR THOSE CLOSE TO YOU AREN'T SUPPORTIVE

Depending on the particular issues your child is facing, you may or may not have problems with family members or those closest to you. If your child has visible physical disabilities, it's much harder for them to deny they have special needs than if they have a condition that doesn't have the same level of external indications. If everyone in your family gets it and you're wrapped up in a cocoon of support, then I'm thrilled for you, and you can skip this chapter. If, however, you've got a spouse, an Aunt Gertie, or a cousin Bob who thinks you are "just coddling that kid of yours" and need to parent harder, well then, Mama, you are in the right spot. Unfortunately, you've also got your work cut out for you.

In my own personal journey, I've had a mix of responses, and you probably will, too. I have always been the primary parent for dropping the kids off and picking them up from daycare and school, so I was the one getting the reports about challenging behavior and issues first-hand. It took my husband a bit to come around and understand fully that we were dealing with something outside of the normal spectrum, even the one for "active little boys." After including him in several of the conversations with Max's teachers, where he could ask his own questions, he came around and has been fully supportive ever since. Luckily, both my mom and my mother-in-law have spent decades in education and understood what we were seeing. I leaned on them both throughout this whole process and am so thankful for them.

Other family members, however, refused to see that there was a legitimate medical problem with my kids, insisting the fault was mine for not parenting harder. And then my friends were hit-or-miss, honestly. Those without kids tried to understand, but can you really grasp anything about parenting when you don't have kids? Not really. And friends with kids either totally got it because they have kids with "quirks" too, or they are sympathetic but still have no clue because their kiddos are neurotypical and they worry about their kids hitting homeruns, not if they're going to have a meltdown during PE and get sent home. Again.

So, I've seen a bit of everything and have drawn not only on my own experiences but also on those of other parents I know. Dealing with people who are close to you is a tricky, tricky business, and you will have to decide who is worth the effort to work with and who, frankly, isn't. You may find you part ways rather dramatically with some people, and other relationships may just wither on the vine as you drift into a new circle of supportive people. In this chapter, I'll talk about three different groups of people (spouses and close family, distant family, and friends) plus some holiday survival tips, because seriously... Holidays. Are. Hard.

In general, I believe people who love you and aren't initially supportive fall into one of two groups: either they don't share the same perspective or education you do on the topic/situation, or they are in denial. When you boil denial down to the underlying base emotion, you usually land on fear. Of the two, education is the easier problem to solve. Fear is a tougher nugget to handle, but I'll try to give you some tips there, too.

If the issue is education, I found it helps to have them get information firsthand from the experts, if possible. You might want to send them a couple of research articles to read, and your child's results from industry-standard testing may go a long way with them. Now, I'm not recommending that you provide testing results to the mailman, but if it's someone you truly need on your team, shoulder-to-shoulder with you, then standard test results may well convince them. Dealing with outright denial driven by fear is trickier. Hell, I was in denial at first myself, so how can I blame anyone else for reacting that way? Often admitting to themselves and others that your child has special needs triggers fears both for the child and their future and for what it means for them personally and their role (especially if they will suddenly be on the hook for increased care demands).

When approaching anyone who is having an emotional response to the news of your child having special needs, it is often helpful to take a step back and remember that your goal here isn't to win an argument. You need to aim toward addressing their underlying fears so they eventually lower their defenses and can at least agree on the support your kiddo needs, even if they still reject the label or diagnosis.

You might even want to share your own fears with someone who is stuck in denial so they feel heard and understood. I might say something like, *"I know this feels overwhelming or like we're just rushing to slap a label on Billy's behavior. I know you love him as much as I do, so I'm guessing you're as scared as I am for what a diagnosis of [XYZ] means for him and for the rest of the family. Labels aside, can we both agree that he needs [ABC] when he's at your house?"* The key here is to validate their feelings and to let them know that you understand where they're coming from, in the hopes of creating a bridge to a less emotionally charged conversation about the specific action or support you need from this family member for your kiddo.

The other thing you may find useful is to shift your conversations away from the diagnosis and instead focus on the specific needs or requests you're making on behalf of your child, the smaller the better in the beginning. For example, *"Henry does best with a consistent routine. It helps him feel supported and stay calm. Please make sure you follow the schedule I'm leaving for you to the best of your ability."* It's less about what kids with this condition/diagnosis need, but what works for your individual child.

When It's a Close Family Member

Many of the suggestions for dealing with a doubting spouse (largely covered in Chapter 4 "Establish Your Foundation") apply here, as well — asking a person to be open, requesting their input, and letting them know you value their questions and perspective should go a long way with anyone, really. But with others outside your nuclear family, you may need to set some boundaries.

If this person is frequently responsible for caring for your child, then the need to get them on board is more critical. Given that you need to make sure they will follow medical protocols and provide consistent behavioral guidelines for your children, you will want to spend the extra effort to convince them you are doing the right, necessary things for your kiddo.

Education will play a large role in getting these family members solidly on your team. I've tried to find a quiet moment where no kiddos are around — meeting for coffee or manicures or just grabbing a glass of wine on the deck while the kids watch a movie — to let them know what my family and child are currently dealing with and how important it is for everyone to support the kiddo through all of it. I've shared my struggles, my fears, all the things I've already tried, the information I've gotten from doctors, teachers, and other experts, along with what is currently working for my little one and how I need this family member to respond. You do have to strike a balance here between giving them as much information as they need without overloading them. Again, this balance point will be different with each person in your extended family, depending on the role they need to play in supporting both your child and **you** going forward.

I'll be honest; I've had mixed success in changing other people's minds about how we're raising our kids and how we deal with their behavior. Once you've done the work of educating and explaining, there may come a time when you realize this other person doesn't agree with you. This is the point where the work turns from convincing them to setting boundaries. Many of the other parents I've spoken with over the years agree — once you've heard people out and considered their input (or not, depending on the source), if they still can't support what your family needs, you've got to be rock solid in your belief that you're doing the right thing no matter what anyone else says.

Your boundaries may look like not allowing a family member to babysit anymore or not discussing your child's situation in detail with them. Remember, boundaries require no action from another party; it's your choice to set and uphold them. I highly encourage you to check out *The Book of Boundaries* by Melissa Urban. Using her framework, you might start by requesting the family member honor your choices for your child, stop bringing up pseudoscience, stop criticizing your parenting, etc. If the behavior persists, then the boundary you set is something like, "I won't let Aunt Sally watch Billy anymore." Or, "I won't stay in a conversation where my parenting is being torn apart."

If the conversation turns to your parenting, you can start out easy with, "I know you would make different choices, but mine aren't up for debate anymore," and then change the subject. If your family member persists, you might need to end the conversation. On the phone, that might sound like, "Aunt Sally, I'm really not going to discuss this with you anymore. We can talk again later." And then hang up. Maybe you leave the texts unread for a while. At Thanksgiving, you might again state your boundary, "I'm not going to entertain further discussion about my parenting choices," and then excuse yourself from the table. Maybe you even leave if it gets that far, but the point is, you're not screaming, "Stop criticizing me!!" (demanding others change their behavior) and flipping over the gravy boat. You're stating, "I won't stay in an overly critical conversation," and then taking all the responsibility for the action/follow-through.

Fundamental disagreements over these matters have taken a toll on my own once-close relationships. It was only after I mourned their loss and stopped trying to "repair" the relationship that I was able to move on. With the help of my therapist, I've been able to change my expectations of interactions with these particular individuals. I don't worry about justifying myself and our family's choices or convincing them I'm doing the right thing when it's just a friend I run into at the grocery store, and I don't worry about it with family members who are determined to be difficult, either. Ultimately, I can't let them matter to me more than my children do. Make no mistake, though, getting your head and heart to this "they don't matter" point will take hard work on your part.

When It's a Family Member You Don't See Often

A doubting or openly critical distant relative is both harder and easier to handle than a close family member. It can be harder for someone who only sees you and your child once or twice a year to really understand what daily life is like for your family. They drop in and out of your life and generally cause a fair amount of disruption to the tenuous routine you cling to, which in turn snowballs into exaggerated behavior (generally of the type you don't want to encourage, right?).

But distant relatives are also a bit easier to handle. You know it's a short time frame that just has to be survived, and then life will go back to normal. In these moments, good enough is freaking awesome — this is when the kids get extra screen time, I don't fight them over eating food they don't want to, and yes, you can have an extra cookie, my love. Do what you have to do to make sure everyone gets out the other side as unscathed as possible. But if someone is really trying to butt in where they don't belong and handing out advice like they won Parent of the Year? Well, for me, this is where I have to be the advocate my kids need me to be, and I've set some boundaries and ground rules and stand firm behind them, rather than trying to convince anyone to come around to my point of view. It's taken me a fair bit of therapy to get to this point, but here's what I do with my own difficult relatives.

I start by spending some time speaking to each relative, one-on-one or in a small group, without the kids around (before the event, if possible), to explain the situation and give them the info they need to get us through the visit at hand. I always hope that this time they'll "get it," but I go in expecting no change from previous interactions with them. It's taken a while for me to really learn this lesson, but Maya Angelou was right when she said, "When someone shows you who they are, believe them the first time." After a few unsuccessful attempts, this looks more like a quick, "Hey, how are you guys? Oh, the kids are good, the therapy I told you about has been helpful, but we still deal a bit with XYZ…" just as a reminder. But I don't go on and on or try to get them to agree with me anymore. I can't keep beating my head against that wall, so I keep it short and simple.

I also prepare my kids for interactions with difficult people. We verbally walk through the entire event and our expectations for behavior and interactions. We pack a bag of well-loved toys and snacks they can pull out and play with if the gathering is light on other kids. Here's where you have to know your own child's triggers so you can coach him on how to respond in different situations. Take the time to walk through everything: Here's how we're going to greet people; here's how we're going to sit at dinner; here's where your safe spot is if you get overwhelmed; here's what I expect you to do if the other kids aren't listening to your words; and so on. I know this sounds like a lot, and it would be awful for my kiddo if I delivered it as a lecture, so I try to just incorporate it into a conversation.

For instance, I might say, *"What are you most excited about for our trip to Nana's? Seeing your cousins? Oh, won't that be fun! I bet they're looking forward to seeing you, too! You know what I've noticed? They really like it when you say hi and then calmly show them the toys you brought. I've noticed it can be scary for them when we come in too excited and they don't get a chance to say hi first before you give them a huge, crunchy hug. Do you think you could use your words first before giving Aiden a hug?"*

This approach helps your child think about the situation at hand in a positive way and understand not only what is appropriate but also what makes other people feel comfortable. If you do nothing else for your child, give him every opportunity to practice interpersonal skills in a guided fashion. Allowing him to have poor personal and social skills because of his disability **does him zero favors**.

Derrick Dufresne, one of the leaders in helping families transition their children from the school system to the public "system," emphasizes this fact in every single speech he gives: "Unless you're rich, you can't afford to be weird." Because like it or not, one day you will be gone, Mama. And you'll need them to have a solid relationship with their cousins or siblings if they will need routine support. So, regardless of how Nana might set your teeth on edge, modeling good personal skills with difficult people and teaching them how to do it as well is critical.

If your kids are older, try asking them to think through the scenarios that might come up and what their different choices might be. Pose the topic to them like one of those old-school Choose Your Own Adventure books some of us had as kids: "If you responded this way, how do you think people would react? What if you made a different choice? Would that change the course of the afternoon at Uncle Bill's?" Let them imagine different scenarios in which they say something mean or make a poor choice, guiding them to see the effect it will have on others and on their enjoyment of the event. Then work together to have a good plan for the situation, especially an escape plan for them if things get tense or weird.

If at all possible, I try to host the event so my kids are on familiar ground. If I can't, then I do a few things to make sure it is as successful as possible. Please remember that with all of these suggestions, you have to know your own kids and family situations and tailor everything to meet your needs. What works for my family and our unique set of special challenges and (challenging) relationships may be the exact opposite of what works for you. My hope is to give you some things to consider, a sense of how I approach situations in my life, and some tools you will find useful for navigating environments that aren't always the most understanding or accommodating.

First, I set expectations with the hosts about how long we'll be staying and whether any accommodations are needed. Second, I make sure to bring lots of toys and snacks that my kids enjoy and will be willing to share with other kids. I keep a close eye on the kids and make sure things are going as well as can be expected. If there is a specific dietary need, I will make sure to contribute a dish that meets it. And third, if it's a short visit (not requiring an overnight stay), I make sure we have an escape plan. We drive separately from the larger group for outings and are not afraid to leave early if necessary.

If it's a longer trip, involving an overnight stay and lots of downtime, I go in with a solid game plan. I refuse to stay with difficult relatives because then we'd be stuck in a tense situation. If anyone asks why I'm not staying at their home, I generally make some polite noises about not wanting to crowd them and feeling it's important to give the kids some space of their own. So I will book us a room at a local hotel and plan some activities. I usually invite the others to go to the zoo/science center/park with us, but if no one else wants to, I'm fine taking my tribe out on my own.

Ultimately, with distant relatives you see infrequently, having low expectations and firm boundaries will be your best course of action. These are people who don't deserve lots of extra time and effort to "bring around," but sometimes you have to interact with them because they're family. Spend some time making sure the environment will be positive for your children, and create a game plan: attractions to visit during free time and activities or toys your children can play with. Remembering that your job is to do what's best for your children and not to appease Great Aunt Milly or your brother's snarky wife will keep you focused on the right things.

When It's a Close Friend

Well, here I've got to wonder how great a person they are if you explain what's going on and they don't understand, or won't try to understand your situation. That being said, I do have friends with whom I definitely don't agree on key topics, but they are still great people, and we can be respectful of each other's viewpoints. Parenting is probably up there on the list of topics that no one ever completely agrees on. My spouse and I are pretty much in sync, and yet we certainly approach parenting issues from different perspectives and would make different decisions from each other if left to our own devices.

So if it's early in the "figuring out what the hell is going on" stage, and you've got a friend who's being unsupportive or who you feel is judging your child's behavior unfairly, you've got a couple of options. You're likely going to have to make this same decision about a lot of people in your life right now: How much do I clue them in before we know exactly what's going on with my kiddo? There will likely be different levels of information you give to groups of people. Random people or casual acquaintances don't deserve much of your precious time right now (if ever). But you may want to bring your close friends into your confidence sooner rather than later.

At this point in the process, you need support, plain and simple. You are confused, scared, and overwhelmed, and the natural human tendency is to retreat and clam up about the less-than-pretty parts of our lives — especially in this Pinterest-mom, social-media-crazy age we live in. Don't retreat. Opening up to your friends will give you space to seek advice, vent to someone outside the situation, and gain perspective.

You need cheerleaders and frequent pep-talks. This road is **hard**, like harder than basic training or moving across the country with a newborn or whatever the hardest thing is you've ever done before. Parenting a child with different needs than others is harder. You will doubt yourself routinely. You will likely doubt yourself daily until you've got your team assembled and support system in place. I would have been a complete hot mess with Henry if I hadn't had both my mom and my mother-in-law on my team, supporting me daily. Their unwavering conviction that we would get everything figured out and resolved, and that I could be the parent my child needed me to be, was a life preserver during a really stormy season. I clung to their advice and words of encouragement with Henry, just like I knew my girlfriend had my back when I was going through the same part of the process with Max.

Assuming you've decided to be open with those who have earned the right to be in your inner circle, and you're getting a weird feeling or a bit of side-eye from someone, take the time to talk to them more in-depth. Follow the same guidelines as above for family and set aside some one-on-one time to bring your friend up to speed. With luck, it will simply be an education issue. She wasn't aware of everything going on, all the things you're dealing with, your concerns, and the implications you're worrying about for your child's future, etc., and once she knows, she's right back to fighting in your corner.

Single, childless friends often have the hardest time fathoming what you're going through because they don't have any frame of reference for it. Those friends may only be able to offer a more casual level of support and may never truly understand what you go through as a special needs mama. The other group I see parents struggle to connect with are friends who have healthy, competitive, or overachieving children, who have tied their own worth to their children's success. You will have to evaluate your relationships with anyone in these two groups and decide, on a case-by-case basis, whether the relationship is worth the effort.

As with every relationship, there will be seasons when you are closer to specific friends and seasons when you pull apart and are less involved in each other's daily lives. The trick for you is to seek out support from your inner circle, but set up some pretty solid boundaries with others. This balance will go a long way toward ensuring you can devote the time and attention required to get your child what she needs, without being distracted by negative people who will only siphon off your limited supply of energy.

Holiday Survival Tips

While a lot of the strategies I've outlined already in this chapter (especially "When It's a Family Member You Don't See Often") certainly apply to holiday gatherings, there are a few additional tips I'd like to share with you. These are things we've learned through years of trial and error. I've tried to pinpoint what made the difference each time we had a trip that was more pleasant than headache. As with everything, you will need to take your own family into consideration before implementing any of them, but I hope they at least provide some food for thought.

First things first: Less is more. Especially if your child is easily over-stimulated, pare down the holidays to the bare minimum that you can. Your child will be getting so much stimulation from the environment outside your home, between everything at the school, to commercials on

TV, to the barrage of holiday-ness in every store from CVS to Target, that you might want to consider taking the family focus down a notch. I find we have fewer holiday meltdowns when we travel less, stay fewer days, accept fewer invitations, decorate less, and do more as a smaller family unit.

Next up, get the kids some exercise and fresh air. This one is on the top of my list, because my two sons have raging ADHD and benefit from expending their energy physically. Their bodies need movement early in the day, so we always plan a hike or a trip to a place where they can run, jump, and play for the morning's activity. Then they're ready for a bit of couch time (so am I, to be honest) and can have good interactions with other people since they've worked their wiggles out beforehand.

Hardest of all for me is letting go of any personal expectations about how perfect the holiday will be. I can get just as sucked up by the Pinterest versions of Thanksgiving as you can, but accepting my holidays will be perfectly imperfect has helped me tremendously. There will be fights, and someone will refuse to eat the entire meal you've prepared. Feelings and toes may be stepped on. The less stress you place on yourself, the more emotionally prepared you'll be to deal with whatever your kiddo and the event throw your way. If you can respond lovingly and thoughtfully to your little person (and others) that will mean more to them (and you) in the long run than any picture-perfect table setting or artfully wrapped present ever will.

In that same vein, be prepared and understanding of the meltdowns that will inevitably happen. I mean, let's be honest here, right? The holidays can make **all** of us a bit crazy, and I've been known to get overwhelmed with it all and need a crying jag followed by either a nap or a hearty glass of wine. Our little ones with special needs are just as susceptible to the tensions, variable schedules, late nights, too much sugar, and anxiety of dealing with Great-Aunt Millie as we are, so do your best to be empathetic and helpful when your kiddo loses his mind and refuses to go, do, eat, say hi, whatever. Do your best to move them along to a preferred activity (AKA distract them! Quick!) and don't make a big deal out of it. This time of year is nuts, and you've just gotta roll with the punches, Mama.

One last thing — take care of yourself, Mama. Go back to Part II on "Sanity-Savers" and use those nervous system navigation tools **liberally** for self-care throughout this whole process and beyond.

CONCLUSION

JUST FOLLOW
THE LANTERNS

Over a decade ago, I walked into Max's elementary school with absolute certainty that my initial request for evaluation was all that was required to get the district to provide the support he needed. Less than an hour later, I had a dramatically different understanding of what we were up against, and I felt completely lost in the dark. I will forever be grateful to my friend from the internet (before that was a thing) for lighting the first lantern to guide my next steps. She got me started, but honestly, when I looked around for the next pool of light, there wasn't one.

In the years since that first pivotal moment, I have relied on my military training, my experience as a negotiator and then entrepreneur, and the practices that have supported my personal healing journey to be the best advocate I can for Max and Henry. Through it all, I kept asking myself, "What about the other mamas just like me? What about their babies? They don't know what I do, and I don't want them to struggle to figure things out like I had to." At first, I poured myself into supporting the local special education community, but it quickly became apparent to me that this book was inside me, waiting to be born.

So, Mama, here we are. I hope you've felt like we were at the kitchen table together while I explained things, and that you heard my voice cheering you on, even as your knees shook. I hope you feel more grounded and confident with the tools and practices that support you in your life just as it is now. I hope you're able to create a high-functioning team that supports your child. I hope all your relationships thrive, with the school, your family, and your community. I hope you refer back to this book and the resources on my website often.

I hope, when you find yourself in the dark middle of figuring something out, that you light a lantern for those who travel behind you.

PART VI

REFERENCES & RESOURCES

GLOSSARY

504 Plan: This is similar to an IEP, but serves a slightly different purpose. A 504 Plan can support a child with any disability, not just the ones defined by IDEA. There is no specialized instruction provided by a 504 Plan. Instead, it works to remove barriers and provide supports in the school environment. Examples of accommodations provided by a 504 Plan: Permitting snacks for a child with diabetes, alternative testing environments, or using audiobooks for children with reading difficulties. A 504 Plan is less formal than an IEP and offers fewer protections. Notably, parental input is not required for the school to change a 504 Plan unilaterally.

Accommodations & Supports: A change in expectations, process, or environment so a person can complete a task. Examples: More time to complete tasks/take tests, movement breaks, assigning fewer problems, moving furniture around so a wheelchair can move freely in a room, allowing a child to have a fidget, or removing handwriting expectations from a child with gross motor movement challenges.

Assistive Technology: This umbrella term refers to anything that supports a child's natural capabilities so they can function and interact with their environment better. Technically, electric lights and eyeglasses count as "assistive technology," so it's something we all use! In general, though, this might refer to things like using a speech-to-text software, a communication board for non-verbal individuals, visual timers, or noise-cancelling headphones.

Case Manager: This term may be used to refer to the Special Education teacher assigned to support your child. In some instances, like where a child is only receiving speech therapy, the case manager might be another specialist, like the speech pathologist. This is the person who should be providing the majority of specialized education and support for your child, and will be your primary point of contact for all things special education for the year.

Co-Taught Classroom: A classroom where there is a team of two teachers supporting all students in the classroom. One is generally the general education teacher who is then partnered with a special education teacher. Both teachers usually work hard not to single children out – this way the ratio of children per teacher drops and everyone (regardless of if they have an IEP/504 Plan or not) can benefit from more personalized instruction and support.

Early Childhood Services: These are tightly defined and limited services available to children up through Kindergarten, usually focused on speech and social/emotional/behavioral supports for children with autism diagnoses.

Early Childhood IEP: In some states, there may be certain educational diagnoses that are only given to children under a certain age. Once a child reaches the maximum age, they can be reevaluated for a school-aged educational diagnosis, which could then result in a school-aged IEP.

Educational Advocate: A person who will advise you on the rights of your child within the education system. They may be a volunteer or charge a fee. Some will attend meetings with the school with you. A good starting place to find a professional, trained advocate is the Council of Parent Attorneys and Advocates at *copaa.org*.

Educational Diagnosis: An educational diagnosis is different than a medical diagnosis. It means that the condition/behaviors present negatively impact a child's ability to learn in the standard general education setting.

A child can have a medical diagnosis of autism spectrum disorder, but not qualify for the same educational diagnosis because it is determined not to be impacting the child at school.

Free and Appropriate Public Education (FAPE): Taken from the Department of Education website, "Students with disabilities have the same right to K-12 public education that students without disabilities have. In order to receive and benefit from that education, students with disabilities may need special education and/or related aids and services. Office for Civil Rights within the U.S. Dept. of Education works to ensure that public elementary and secondary schools, including charter schools, provide a free appropriate public education (FAPE) to all qualified students with disabilities (generally, students with disabilities who are of school age), regardless of the nature or severity of their disabilities. Section 504 and Title II require public schools to provide appropriate education and modifications, aids, and related services free of charge to students with disabilities and their parents or guardians. The "appropriate" component means that this education must be designed to meet the individual educational needs of the student as determined through appropriate evaluation and placement procedures. However, students with disabilities must be educated with students without disabilities to the maximum extent appropriate."

General Education Classroom: Refers to classrooms where the standard education curriculum is presented to students using uniform teaching methods. Also known as a regular classroom.

Individuals with Disabilities Education Act (IDEA): The federal law that requires public schools to provide a Free Appropriate Public Education (FAPE) to eligible children with disabilities.

Individualized Education Program (IEP): An IEP is a legally binding document defining a plan or program created to ensure that a child with a disability identified under the law and attending an elementary or secondary school receives specialized instruction and related services.

IEP Goals: These are formally documented, standards-based goals aimed to measure the effectiveness of the specialized instruction being provided to a child.

IEP Process: The formal process for requesting specialized education, evaluating a child for one of the disabilities defined under current state and federal law, and determining what the plan is to support the child if they are found to be eligible for an IEP. This is generally accomplished in a series of meetings between a variety of school and district staff, the child's parents, and, optionally, the child themselves.

Intellectual Disability: A neurodevelopmental disorder characterized by significant limitations in practical and conceptual skills and mental capacity.

Learning Disability: A neurodevelopmental disorder that affects a person's ability to learn, retain, and use information. Learning disabilities are not to be confused with intellectual disabilities or behavioral issues.

Medical Diagnosis: A health condition identified by a doctor outside the public school system, i.e., ADHD or autism spectrum disorder. A medical diagnosis does not automatically mean a child will qualify for educational eligibility under IDEA.

Meditation: A specific and structured activity that aims to foster greater clarity of thought and a calm mental and spiritual state. Usually performed while still, either seated or lying down. Meditation requires mindfulness; however, mindfulness does not require one to practice meditation.

Mindfulness: A broad state of being present, aware, and judgement-free of the current moment, including one's thoughts, emotions, and physical state. Mindfulness is a lifelong practice that can be achieved while doing other activities, like hiking, gardening, or doing the dishes.

Para-Educator: May also be referred to as a Paraprofessional or teacher's aide. This staff member works to support teachers and students in the classroom, often focusing specifically on students with special needs. This person has likely received some degree of training, but may not be a fully licensed teacher.

Parent Advisory Council (PAC): The name for a parent-run organization focused on supporting the families of children who receive special education services. This group is not mandated to exist (in most places) and since it is parent-run, it can have a wide variety of names, charters, areas of focus, and wildly different levels of support from school and district administration.

Private-Pay Provider: A medical provider who does not work with any insurance companies to receive payment. A client/patient must pay out-of-pocket for these services, and the amount paid will not count towards any deductible or out-of-pocket maximums as calculated by your health insurance company.

Reiki: An energetic healing practice originating in Japan, Reiki means "universal life force." In other traditions, this life force is called prana, ka, chi, or even the Holy Spirit. In Reiki, one who has been trained by a Reiki Master taps into this universal life force and channels its healing powers for themselves or others. Receiving Reiki is a very relaxing experience, leaving most people with a deep sense of calm and stress relief. Reiki can be done either in person or virtually. Reiki has slowly gained awareness and acceptance in Western culture, to the point where it is now offered as a restorative treatment at many major cancer centers, including the Mayo Clinic.

Sensory Room: A contained room filled with items that support nervous system regulation, often a quiet place with fidgets and other items providing a variety of sounds, textures, movement, and pressure on the body.

Somatics: A group of therapeutic practices that focus on the body and its wisdom as a way of improving mental and physical health, honoring that the mind and body are one interconnected system. Somatic methods include breathwork, visualization, somatic experiencing, Emotional Freedom Technique/Tapping, ecstatic movement/dance, vagus nerve toning/stimulation, and sound healing.

Special Education: Specialized instruction provided to support students with disabilities or special needs. In most instances, providing special education is the responsibility of the public school district in which you reside.

Special Education Classroom: A classroom focused on providing individualized and specialized instruction for children with disabilities. All students in these classrooms have IEPs that dictate how much of a child's day shall be spent in a special education environment vs. the general education classroom/environment, up to and including a child's full-time placement in the special education setting. It can also be called as a "self-contained" classroom.

Special School District (SSD) of St. Louis: This organization overlays all 22 school districts in St. Louis County and is responsible for providing special education services to every qualifying child in the county. Children are students first and foremost of their home district (i.e. Kirkwood School District) and receive their services from an SSD staff member who is placed within the home district or school. SSD is one of the very few in the entire country structured this way, but since I'm anticipating quite a few readers from my region, I felt it is worth mentioning.

RESOURCES AVAILABLE AT WWW.REBEGOEBEL.COM/ BOOKRESOURCES

- Guided Meditations
- Worksheets for each IEP meeting
- Parent Organizer: New School Year Transition Guide
- Links to Helpful Resources (organizations, books, websites, etc.)
- Access to a community of other parents like you

IEP MEETING MAP & OVERVIEW

Meeting Name	Meeting purpose
Evaluation or Review of Existing Data or Domain Meeting	To determine whether evaluations are to be done.
Results or Eligibility Meeting	To review the results of the completed evaluations and determine Eligibility for an IEP.
IEP Meeting	To set the goals and decide what accommodations, modifications, and assistive technology will be part of the child's IEP.
IEP Review Meeting	Every IEP must be reviewed and updated at least annually, but can be updated more frequently if needed.

	Evaluation or Review of Existing Data Meeting
Meeting Purpose	To determine whether testing is to be done.
Bring with You	The Evaluation Meeting Parent Organizer, found at *http://www.rebegoebel.com/bookresources,* along with copies of any external reports/diagnoses and a consolidated list of issues or behaviors you've observed at home, plus any other concerns you have.
Know Before Leaving	What is the decision of the team (to test or not to test). What are the exact names of the tests to be performed (if any). Who is your point of contact going forward and how to reach them. A list of Parent Resources available to you through your school district.
Your Homework	Before the next meeting, Google each of the test names you were given. Take notes so you understand at a high level what the test is looking for, what "average" scores look like and what higher and lower scores mean.

	Results or Eligibility Meeting
Meeting Purpose	To share the results of the testing performed and determines if the data indicates eligibility for your state has been met, therefore requiring an IEP.
Bring with You	The notes you took when you looked up all the tests, along with copies of any new external reports/diagnoses.
Know Before Leaving	The results of every single test they gave your child, the decision of the team is (does your child qualify for special services and require an IEP), when the next meeting will be held and the purpose of it. You should also be given a written report that goes over all this in detail, along with the decision either at the meeting or within a day or two afterwards.
Your Homework	Before the next meeting, go over all the results again. Google them if you don't understand at a high level what they're telling you. Also, think about what the goals you have are for your child. Your next meeting will be to set out these goals and the aids the school will provide to achieve them. More on Goal Writing/Setting in "Writing IEP Goals."

	IEP Meeting
Meeting Purpose	To write the Individualized Education Program for your child, including goals and methods of measurement for each area of concern.
Bring with You	Any thoughts you have on goals for the areas of concern you discussed as a team during the Results Meeting, or any concerns and questions that may have come up as you and your partner have discussed things.
Know Before Leaving	What the goals are, how they will be measured, who will be doing the measuring, how often you'll get updates on progress.
Your Homework	None, besides staying in communication with the team and ensuring you receive the progress updates as agreed upon.

	IEP Update or Review Meeting
Meeting Purpose:	To Review the IEP for your child and make updates as necessary.
Bring With You:	Any thoughts you have on both the current goals and suggestions for new age-appropriate goals to add.
Know Before Leaving:	What the new or updated goals are, how they will be measured, who will be doing the measuring, and how often you'll get updates.
Your Homework:	None, besides maintaining regular communication with the team and reviewing scheduled updates on goals.

NEGOTIATION/MEETING PREPARATION WORKSHEET

For a discussion of how to fill this out, check out "Negotiation." If you'd like a blank, printable version of the Negotiation/Meeting Preparation worksheet, visit the Book Resources on my website.

Key Topic/ Goal/ Decision to be made	Topic #1	Topic #2
What is my best-case outcome for this item?		
What do I think the school wants to happen here?		
What is my minimum acceptable solution? My walk-away point?		
What rank is this on my priority list?		
Do I need more information on this topic?		
Questions to ask about this topic		
Outcome		

SAMPLE Negotiation Worksheet

Key Topic/ Goal/ Decision to be made	Topic #1 (EXAMPLE): Get Max evaluated for special needs	Topic #2
What is my best-case outcome for this item?	Max gets the full battery of evaluations necessary to figure out what is going on and how to tailor his education and the teaching methods so that we unlock the highest potential he has	
What do I think the school wants to happen here?	The school would rather not provide the resources for expensive evaluations due to a severe state-wide budget crunch. They want to wait until Max is failing until performing evaluations and committing to an IEP and the resources needed to fulfill one.	
What is my minimum acceptable solution? My walk-away point?	The minimum I'm willing to accept is evaluations for ADHD, Speech, and a Learning Disability. I know this is what he needs. I'm willing to fight to guarantee this outcome.	
What rank is this on my priority list?	Number One—nothing is more important.	
Do I need more information on this topic?	I'm not sure what other evaluations are available or are appropriate for the signs we've been seeing in Max.	

Key Topic/ Goal/ Decision to be made	Topic #1 (EXAMPLE): Get Max evaluated for special needs	Topic #2
Questions to ask about this topic	- What are the other evaluations that would be appropriate to complete at this time to give us the fullest picture of what we're dealing with here and how to best help Max? - What will we learn from each evaluation? - What is the exact name of each evaluation to be performed (so we can Google it later)? - If a specific evaluation is rejected, why? - Etc.	
Outcome	** If you bring this worksheet with you, fill this block out as you go along. One, you'll look so prepared it sends a strong message to the others in the room that you are #uneffwithable. And two, this allows you to recap all the decisions made at the end of the meeting to make sure everyone is on the same page. Win-win!	

Recommended Reading

Wrightslaw: From Emotions to Advocacy, by Pam and Pete Wright
Parenting with Love and Logic, by Foster Cline and Jim Fay
The Book of Boundaries, by Melissa Urban

ACKNOWLEDGMENTS

I SIMPLY MUST BEGIN WITH THANKING my husband, Alex. I know spouses are typically listed last, but without his steady love in my life, I wouldn't be the woman I am today, with the wisdom and experience necessary to light these lanterns for you. He has spent many hours by my side, first advocating for our children, and then reading drafts or listening to me talk through parts of this book again and again. Your support and encouragement to dust this manuscript off after a five-year hiatus and turn it into a book, which I now get to hold in my hands, were instrumental. Thanks for being the spreadsheet to my woo, Babe. Together, we make a pretty kick-ass team.

I have equal gratitude for my children, Max and Henry. They're both old enough to know what I'm writing about and have provided their consent to share the stories contained within this book. You guys are such amazing young men, and it's been my honor to walk beside you, fight for you, and watch you grow up. Thanks for choosing me as your mama and making me laugh with your shenanigans. I love you to the moon and back.

To the women who have illuminated parts of my path – thank you. Amy, we became friends on the internet before that was a thing, and you helped me challenge that first "no" from the school and learn how to advocate for my babies. You altered the trajectory not only of my children's lives but also of my own, and now, through this book, the lives of many other children. Your kindness will ripple throughout a generation (and this will surprise exactly no one who has the pleasure of knowing you).

Jamie, I've said it before, but I still don't know how you and I became friends after you were Henry's kindergarten teacher. What a wild ride. You are a talented and dedicated educator who cares deeply about every single child that comes through your classroom. Your encouragement and friendship, not to mention your services as an advisor and the copy editor of this book, have been solid parts of my foundation over the last ten years. I look forward to being old ladies together as we celebrate life's coming milestones.

To the women who continually guide me back to myself, Timea and Sadie, thank you for being such amazing examples of embodied leadership. Thank you for going first, figuring it out, and lighting your own set of lanterns for me to follow. The lessons I've learned from each of you are indelible – written on my soul – and have not only changed me for the better, but they were also the missing piece of *Lanterns in the Dark* that I needed before I could finish writing it. Your impact on the lives of the people you coach is immeasurable. Thank you.

Thank you to the myriad of friends who have encouraged me and shaped this book over the years in ways large and small: Angela, Adina, Jazmin, Jenny, Lexie, Megan, Melissa, Molly, Paola, Rebekah, Teri, and others whom I'm sure I've unintentionally forgotten to mention.

Thank yous go out to my developmental editor, Dawn Raffel, who helped guide this book through two completely different iterations, and to Jon Hahn for the cover and interior design. I'd also like to recognize the St Louis Writers' Guild and the St Louis Publishers' Association for the amazing support they provide to authors in our region.

Lastly, to the rest of my family, thank you for the support, pep talks, meals, listening ears, shoulders to cry on, and belief that I could absolutely do what I set out to do – raise good young men and write this damn book. Both my parents and my parents-in-law have had a hand in shaping the woman I am today, and I'm beyond grateful for their love.

ABOUT THE AUTHOR

REBE GOEBEL is the mama of kiddos with special needs, just like you. She is also a trauma-informed Parent Advocacy Coach who specializes in helping parents navigate the special education system without sacrificing their own physical and mental health. Her approach is rooted in the belief that effective advocacy requires a strategic knowledge of the system, strong leadership skills, and—most importantly—a grounded nervous system as the foundation.

Rebe's journey began over a decade ago when her first foray into special education ended in what she describes as a "shocking disaster". Realizing her son couldn't afford for her to be a passive participant, she drew on her experience as an Air Force officer and a corporate contract negotiator to secure the support he needed. This experience led to a pivotal realization: a parent's nervous system sets the tone for every interaction, from the living room to the IEP table.

Today, Rebe leverages decades of leadership experience alongside certifications in somatic work, including trauma-informed breathwork and Reiki energy healing. She graduated Summa Cum Laude from the University of Missouri, where she met her husband, Alex.

When she isn't lighting lanterns for other mamas, Rebe can be found in the St. Louis area cheering on her two teenage sons at wrestling matches and lacrosse games. In her quieter moments, she is often found with a mug of tea and a good book. An avid traveler, she is happiest with her toes in the surf.

To explore Rebe's current offerings, including coaching packages, workshops, and courses, visit her online at www.rebegoebel.com or on Instagram @rebegoebel.